Surviving Your First Year
as Pastor

Surviving Your First Year as Pastor

What Seminary Couldn't Teach You

Angie Best-Boss

Judson Press
Valley Forge

Surviving Your First Year as Pastor:
What Seminary Couldn't Teach You
© 1999 by Judson Press, Valley Forge, PA 19482-0851
All rights reserved.

Library of Congress Cataloging-in-Publication Data
Best-Boss, Angie.
   Surviving your first year as pastor : what seminary couldn't
teach you / Angie Best-Boss.
       p.   cm.
ISBN 0-8170-1300-8 (pbk.)
1. Church management. 2. Clergy—Office. 3. Church work.
I. Title.
BV652.B47 1999
253—DC21   98-49773

Printed in the U.S.A.
06 05 04 03 02 01 00 99
5 4 3 2 1

To my husband, DuWain, and daughter, Kaylyn,
who have loved me and taught me how to love;

And to Colony Friends and
Anderson First Friends Meetings,
who have loved me and taught me how to pastor.

Contents

Acknowledgments

With grateful appreciation to

Sarah Houston, Nan Jenkins, and Sharon Carrow
for loving support,

Dr. William Lockwood, for being such a faithful mentor,

and Karen Finley, for editing and encouragement.

The Church Is Different from Seminary

A legend has been around for a while that says a young new pastor came to a small town in Georgia right out of seminary. He was full of excitement and enthusiasm and couldn't wait to get started. So before the moving van was even unpacked, he walked across the street to get his first glimpse of his new Methodist church.

It was a beautiful old church, rich with history, and it looked warm and inviting. However, the first thing that the pastor noticed was an old, gnarled tree that blocked the side doors of the building. He frowned and thought, "Not only is that tree ugly; it is a fire hazard as well. Why hasn't someone done something about it?" Then he decided that a great way to take initiative would be to cut down the tree as a surprise for his members on Sunday morning.

In short order, the tree was down. Unfortunately, he had not realized that the tree was supposed to have been planted by Methodism's founder, John Wesley, hundreds of years earlier. The young pastor never had to unpack his boxes; he never even made it to Sunday morning. He was asked to leave less than forty-eight hours after he had arrived.

Is the story true? No one knows. But the reality that is behind the story is. If pastors come to their new churches and begin acting without any idea of who their members are and what's important to the church, then they are doomed from the start. New pastors need to have a good understanding of the congregation's goals and of their own responsibilities in accomplishing those goals.

In many ways, seminary is different from the local church. Seminary consists primarily of three intense years of studying, reading, and brief internships in the church. It is a more independent process than the local church requires. Papers, exams, and projects are usually graded on individual work, with little opportunity to work with groups of people in developing projects. Nevertheless, a pastor who cannot operate within a team will not see many long-term pastorates.

Seminary has a definite rhythm to it. Semesters rise and fall, beginning with the passing out of syllabi and ending with final exams and papers. Winter and summer sessions come and go; new classes start and end in just a few months. Assignments are given, then completed. The schedule never changes. You can depend on it.

Rarely does life in a church feel that way. As soon as one sermon is completed, the next has to be prepared. While church seasons like Advent and Lent dictate a certain amount of activity and programming needs, many projects have no such timetable. They may linger for months in committee sessions and board meetings. Congregation members will have the same problems for months and years, all the while ignoring your well-thought-out advice that you know will be helpful, if they will just follow it.

Perhaps most importantly, one of the biggest differences between seminary and pastoral life will be your focus. While the hours spent discussing liberation theology and conjugating Greek verbs may have been enlightening, parish life is much less focused on academics and more focused on the nitty-gritty details of administering a church and taking care of the needs of your people. While seminary focuses on academics, the pastorate is focused on your people. Frequently, the most important theological term most of your members will need to hear is that Jesus loves them.

Hopefully, the biggest difference between your seminary experience and your first pastorate in the local church will be the job satisfaction and fulfillment that you receive in the church. As enjoyable as seminary education can be, it can't hold a candle to being given the opportunity to participate in some of the most intimate, heartbreaking, and wonderful moments in people's lives. For that opportunity, we, as pastors, should be grateful. It is what brings us joy.

CHAPTER 1

Be Prepared
Know What You're Getting Into

The moving van was being unpacked. While I was putting away dishes, we turned on the television in a desperate attempt to amuse our preschooler and keep her out of harm's way. Within a few minutes, I heard sirens in the distance. Thinking little of it, I assumed it was the fire station and went back to unwrapping glasses. Shortly, an announcer came on the television, saying that our community was under a "Tornado Watch" and that we should take necessary tornado precautions.

Not having any idea what such precautions would be, I walked into the den, hoping for more information. The newscaster just smiled and shook his head, saying, "This is what we get, folks, for living in the middle of Tornado Alley." My mind began racing. "Tornado Alley? What is that? I've never heard of that before. No one mentioned a Tornado Alley to me in the sales pitch. I'm sure I would have remembered that piece of information!"

That was the first time, but not the last, that I realized I had not gathered all the information I needed about my first church out of seminary. Because I didn't know what questions to ask, and because the church didn't want to present all of its difficulties and portray a gloomy picture, I was not prepared for some of the surprises that awaited me when I arrived at my first church.

For example, over the previous year, the church had depleted their reserve fund of more than ten thousand dollars. Because of a great deal of conflict regarding the former pastor's resignation, the congregation was both discouraged and rapidly diminishing; they had very little money in reserve. Had I requested copies of their monthly financial statements over the past year, I would not have been so surprised at my first business meeting.

While many denominations allow pastors to be hired by individual congregations, several denominations still have district superintendents, presiding bishops, or other church leaders who place pastors. Regardless of the placement method your church employs, the more information you gather before you arrive and within the first few months, the better prepared you will be.

The three most important types of information you need are your church's history, its current situation, and facts about the community in which it is located. This information is intended, not to be used to make a judgment call about whether to pastor there or not, but as an indicator of red flags around particular issues or events. For example, if the church has gone through ten pastors in fifteen years, that fact probably needs to be investigated. You may still feel led to pastor there, but it is helpful to know more information about the troubling statistic, especially if you can find out some of the reasons for the high turnover.

How do you get information? Start with denominational yearbooks, if available, or make inquiries through the denominational headquarters. That office can generally provide information on attendance, membership, church history, former pastors, and payment of denominational dues, if applicable. The denomination's area representative may also be a helpful source of information on a wide variety of topics.

As well, questions can be asked formally of a board with whom you're meeting to interview or informally as you talk with and get to know its members. Typically members are not reluctant to tell you about their experiences in the church and their concerns. I usually ask, "Have you been in the church long?" and that often gets the conversation started.

It might also be helpful to ask people in the community if they have ever heard of the church and what their perceptions are. When my husband and I pulled into town with our moving van, we met an unexpected roadblock, and we got lost. We stopped at several places to ask for directions and found that no one had ever heard of the church, even though most places were less than three miles away. That observation gave me a fairly accurate indication of the church's involvement in community life.

Discover the Church's History

First, find out about where this church has been. Each church has its own particular story that has helped shape its members and its traditions. This is an important part of its legacy. However, getting to know a church's story is an ongoing process that takes years to understand. You cannot learn its entire history in a few hours, but you can begin picking up pieces of the puzzle. As pastor, you will continue to hear the church's story unfold, but getting a sense of its history lets you begin to learn where the congregation has been.

Some sample questions to ask include:

- Why was the church started?
- By whom was it started?
- Did it always meet in its current location?
- Has attendance decreased or increased in the past five years?
- How frequently has the church changed pastors?
- Has the church membership ever split? If so, over what issue(s)?
- Of what is the congregation most proud?
- What is the biggest obstacle they have overcome?
- When have they felt defeated?
- What are the church's best traditions?

Discover the Church's Mission

Every church does something well. Each church can claim something as being unique to it. It may host fantastic barbecue dinners, cultivate a strong youth program, or fund missionaries well. You probably won't have to dig too deeply to uncover the congregation's pride and joy. At the same time, you will also want to scratch the surface and dig for more information about the church's current state. I always found it helpful to ask members about their mission statement, not just about its formal wording but about how it has been lived out.

Some questions to consider include:

- What is the church's greatest asset?
- What is the greatest challenge it is now facing?
- What impact does the church have, and/or want to have, on the community?
- What does the congregation want in a pastor?
- Do they have a job description for this leader?
- What is the church's current financial state? (i.e., amount of debt, in reserve, etc.)
- Why is there a need for a pastoral transition?
- What is the current average attendance?
- Describe the congregation. (i.e., demographics, involvement, personality, etc.)

If possible, ask for copies of the church bulletin, newsletter, administrative board reports and financial statements, preferably for the last twelve months. When I accepted my first call to pastor a church, I asked to be placed on the mailing list so when I arrived three months later, the prayer concerns, business issues, and coming events were not brand-new.

Within a few weeks or months after you arrive, you may find it interesting and enlightening to spend a few days poring over board minutes from previous years. The process is tedious but well worth the time involved. You may pick up on sacred cows or recent issues you might have missed otherwise.

For example, I discovered that my church had bad experiences with two different pictorial directories. Pictures were lost, the directories were never completed, and people wasted a great deal of time and effort. In light of this history, I decided not to resurrect the idea too quickly in my ministry there. While I think such directories are a great ministry tool, I know my congregation will have to wait several more years before the bitter taste leaves their mouths and they will agree to try one again.

Discover the Church's Setting

You will want to find out in what kind of community the church is located, particularly if it is in a part of the country with which you're not familiar. Take as much time as you can to get to know the area. If you are interviewing for the position, arrange to stay for a few days to visit the community. Try to avoid coming in for just one night and a Sunday morning. Quite frankly, a Sunday morning visit is almost not worth the trip. The decision is too important to make without as much information as possible.

If you can, take your family with you. I learned this the hard way. I had been to several churches and taken my family with me to all of them. After the first couple of churches, we decided that traveling with a child was just too difficult, and so I would go alone and my husband would trust my decision. However, in the end, we decided that we didn't want to make the decision without my husband having seen the church. So we had to make a second trip to the churches in which we were interested. Even if you are placed in a church by denominational leaders, a chance to look at schools, stores, and nearby neighborhoods makes the transition easier for everyone in the family.

If someone offers to loan you a car while you are in town, accept. Grab a map and drive off the well-beaten paths. That way you can be sure you are not being driven through only the nicest areas and bypassing a dilapidated downtown where you would have to do most of your shopping.

Even though it may be tempting to stay in a hotel, accept

any offers to stay in members' homes. You will get to know people better and learn much more about the church and its current situation. Read the newspapers; listen to the local news; eat at mom-and-pop restaurants; do anything you can to get a sense of what it means to live there.

Stop by the chamber of commerce for brochures as well as demographic information. Not only can you find out about special attractions like museums and amusements parks, but you will learn a lot about who the residents are. Ask questions like:

- Has the population been decreasing or increasing in the last few years?
- Are there many single-parent homes?
- Is the largest population over sixty-five?
- What is the area's median income?
- Who are the biggest employers?

This information will be especially helpful in allowing you as the new pastor to better discern the needs of the community.

Knowing the community is also important when considering the needs of your family. I candidated at one church that was downtown in a major metropolitan center. Because the public school was in such upheaval, we had to consider the cost, distance, and availability of a private-school education for our daughter. Other considerations may include available job opportunities for your spouse. In a rural community, that may prove to be a major concern.

Discuss Your Salary

Make sure you understand the pastor's compensation package. Ask for it in writing. A simple cash salary for pastors is rare. Call your denomination's headquarters and ask for assistance in understanding the basics in your denomination. Several denominations offer salary guidelines that are useful in determining what can generally be expected. However, in others, the larger church body sets the salary guidelines for its local churches.

One of the biggest concerns is housing. Is the parsonage adequate for your family? Are all utilities included, or are there some—like the telephone or cable television—for which you will be responsible? Will you be given extra income to build equity in a home? Housing allowances are becoming more and more popular.

Increasingly, many churches also offer a parsonage allowance. This is a tax-free way to supplement your salary, but it can only be used for renter's insurance and items for your home such as cleaning supplies, furniture, cable TV, firewood, landscaping, and linens. The IRS limits how much of your income can be paid in this way, and Social Security does have to be paid on this income.

Some churches pay for their pastor's Social Security, but many do not. Most pastors are self-employed and have to pay their own taxes and Social Security quarterly. Worker's compensation benefits, which pay if someone is injured on the job, vary from state to state, but the laws sometimes exempt churches.

The pastor's compensation should also include payment toward a pension. Additional benefits often include a car allowance. Some churches pay a set amount each month, and others pay based on monthly mileage. Ask about a professional expense account also; it is helpful for covering costs associated with attending denominational meetings and conferences, purchasing job-related books, and paying professional organizational dues. Health insurance for your family should be part of your compensation, whether through your denomination or an independent policy you find for yourself. If you obtain your own policy, make sure you get a price quote so you are ready when you negotiate your salary. Health coverage may include maternity, dental, eye, and preventive care.

You also need to determine how much vacation time is available and if you will be allowed time off to attend conferences and other professional events and if it will be paid. In larger churches, sick days may also be included. While salaries are often nonnegotiable, there is frequently some flexibility concerning vacation time and other benefits.

This is not an exhaustive list of all considerations, but it is a start. You may find it helpful to sit down with another pastor in your new community; she or he can help you get a good grasp of what to expect from your experience in your geographical area and in your denomination.

Most importantly perhaps, sit down with your family before you begin the candidating process and decide what kind of salary you need for your family's lifestyle. Don't forget about paying school loans and self-employment tax. While pastor's compensation is often found in many nonmaterial ways, you do have a responsibility to provide basic needs for your family and to stay out of debt.

In the End

There is some information about beginning a new church that you do *not* need. Some people will want to tell you who is most likely to steal from the mission funds or nose through the pastor's desk and who is *least* likely to donate a dollar for doughnut fellowship. These things you do not need to know. People deserve the opportunity to begin their relationship with you with a clean slate.

Gathering all of this information (while avoiding gossip) may seem like an incredible task. It does require some effort. Nevertheless, it is far better to work more diligently now than to walk into an explosive situation that you could have been better prepared for.

A fellow pastor once accepted a church without asking why the last two pastors had left in only two years. When he arrived, he found that a former beloved pastor who had served for thirty-nine years was still actively involved and informally acted as senior pastor in many ways. What the search committee really wanted was someone to ask the retired pastor to step back into a more passive role. Unfortunately, no one mentioned this dilemma until after my colleague had begun as the pastor. To no one's surprise, he lasted only three years.

Even when all the information is in, however, the decision about where to pastor has to be based on the Lord's call in your life. Some pastors know immediately where God wants them to be, while others have to make difficult decisions, carefully weighing all of the information and praying for wisdom. Regardless, all new pastors need to enter their church with as much information as possible so they can be equipped to serve God's people in that place. Being informed helps us become good stewards of that which God has entrusted to our care.

Resources

Nolan B. Harmon, *Ministerial Ethics and Etiquette.* Abingdon Press, 1987.

Christopher Moore, *Opening the Clergy Parachute: Soft Landings for Church Leaders Who Are Seeking a Change.* Abingdon Press, 1995.

CHAPTER 2

First Things First
Taking One Step at a Time

Your Family's Needs

Remember that your first priority is taking care of your family. Especially during the first few weeks, take time to be attentive to their needs, and don't neglect to take your days off. While you may be excited and raring to get to work, be sensitive to your spouse and children, who may not be ready to tackle a new city on their own. The loss of family and friends combined with the seemingly overwhelming task of making a new place feel like home can be stressful.

Each family's needs are different, so be sensitive to yours. For our daughter, we decided that after we had settled in, we would go to the humane society and get a kitten. You may not want to add a new pet to your family, but it is fun to have something for everyone to anticipate.

Planning a special activity soon after the move will also help. Look for a zoo, playground, or museum nearby. Even a trip to the library or shopping mall during the first week will help children get used to a new situation. Or on Sunday afternoon after church, bring along a picnic lunch, a map, and a spirit of adventure. Take a driving tour of your town and surrounding neighborhoods for a few hours.

Start having the newspaper delivered daily as soon as possible. It is worth the expense to be aware of what is happening in your community. Not only will you find out about local activities and cultural events; you will also be up-to-date on local news that affects your members. Be on the lookout for local employment changes, obituaries, awards and honors, and other events that your community will expect you to be aware of.

Generally, pastoral changes happen in the summer, so the weather is often pleasant, and there may be a number of activities going on in the community. Look for county fairs, craft shows, or any other gatherings in which your family might be interested.

Taking pictures or creating a special video for out-of-town family members and friends is another fun activity during the first few weeks. Let children be the tour guide, deciding what pictures to take and what to say about them. It will be appreciated by those who miss you and fun to do, and it will be a good opportunity for your own family to process feelings and thoughts about their new home.

The Church's Needs

When you are ready to tackle church work, it is often difficult to decide where to begin. The first thing to do is call the leader of your administrative body or other appropriate person and ask if anyone is ill, in the hospital, or in any other type of crisis situation that needs your immediate attention. If you have a church secretary, she or he will probably know current situations as well. Getting in a pastoral visit or two in the first week will be noticed and appreciated by your congregation.

It is tempting to want to organize your office and put away all your books and settle in your office. Don't; there is plenty of time for that. Set your office hours, publish them in the bulletin, and begin the following week. Many pastors take Monday off; the days they are in the office, they work from nine o'clock A.M. until noon and then visit in the afternoon. Find a schedule that works for you, but be sensitive to the schedule to which your congregation is accustomed.

I found that when I worked at maintaining my published office hours, people were more likely to come by for a visit. While many members would never have called to make an appointment for "counseling," they felt comfortable dropping in just to talk. Being in your office for regular hours opens up your door for ministry.

Try to be interruptible as much as possible. People come before administrative responsibilities. Don't count on being able to work on your sermon every morning. Between phone calls and unexpected visitors, I consider it a bonus if I have time to write my sermon in the mornings. Instead, I visit three afternoons a week and work on my sermon on the other two afternoons. My mornings are free to spend on administrative tasks, correspondence, and telephone calls.

Getting to Know Them

The most important thing you will be doing during your first year of ministry in the church is building relationships with your members. Nothing else matters nearly as much. Even in a small congregation, your members will come from a wide variety of backgrounds and experiences. Spending time with your congregation is critical so that you can be a better pastor.

Be where the people are. If the church plays softball or families have open houses, then be there. Look for ways to let your members know you are interested in who they are. Attend their children's recitals, athletic events, and other special events as time allows. Some pastors have Sunday school classes or other small groups in their homes for fellowship times. Others invite a family at a time to dinner or host an annual open house.

During those first few months, your members will be watching you to see if you keep your word. They will be listening to you, determining if you are compassionate and trustworthy. They will be talking with one another about you, trying to get a clearer picture of who you are. It is important to be a good shepherd at all stages of your pastoral life, but no other time is more crucial than these initial weeks and months. People will be making judgments about you early in your ministry that may be difficult to change later.

Pastors must find the fine line between being pastoral and being pushy. You must earn the right to be their pastor. Spend as much time as possible getting to know your members, but remember that it takes time to build new relationships, especially one as personal as the one between a pastor and a congregation.

Allowing Them to Know You

Not only do you have to get to know your congregation, but they also need the opportunity to get to know you. The members probably already know a lot of facts about you from your resume and earlier meetings with them. While they may know where you are from, where you received your education, and how many children you have, there is a lot of important information that they don't know yet. Being aware of their need to know helps you to be intentional in revealing the desired information.

For example, your members need to know some of what makes you, *you*. What has your spiritual journey been like? What have some of your struggles been? your joys? As you get to know one another, your members will need to hear more about what has shaped your life. Look for ways to incorporate telling your story to your members.

The easiest way to do this is through church publications such as the newsletter. Spend some time writing about who you are and from where you come. When the newsletter was due out on my first Sunday, I wrote a quick story about our nightmare moving trip. It was a nice way to break the ice because many families could relate. When I talked about having a child with a bladder the size of a pea and the mixed emotions we felt pulling out of the driveway at our previous home, they knew a little bit more about our family.

With my family members' permission, I often tell discreet personal stories in my sermon about our family life. Look for ways to incorporate your personal experiences in ways that relate to the theme being addressed. People respond positively because it is another connection being made, even if it just triggers memories of their own. Frequently, people will say that telling a story from my own life has helped them understand an abstract point.

When you are visiting with members of the congregation, look for ways to tell them about your life. However, remember not to say anything personal that you would not want told from the pulpit or in the newsletter. Expect members to talk to one another about you and your family. Overall, they care about you and want to get to know you and your family better. I find that older members in particular, like to hear stories about my children. It often brings back special memories for them and helps make me seem more real and down-to-earth.

Be aware that your members' feelings toward you may be further complicated by their feelings toward the former pastor. Consequently, some members of the congregation may feel that they are being disloyal if they are friendly to you right away. Others might even be angry at you for being in your position because they were not in favor of a pastoral change. There is nothing you can do except be available, but it helps to know that the criticism isn't personal. In time, preconceptions and prejudices fade. I had been pastor for about a year before one woman revealed, "You know, I didn't want to like you. I was mad at you for taking the place of the former pastor. But even though I miss him, I'm glad you are here."

To Change or Not to Change

One of the most important things to remember in the early days of your ministry is not to come in and make changes right away. Changes, if necessary, can come later. The single greatest mistake new pastors make is to come sweeping into their new churches like missionaries to pagan heathens and begin making changes left and right with little understanding of how that particular church operates. Lone Ranger ministers don't last long.

Granted, there are times in the life of a church when changes will have to be made immediately, but it is surprising how rarely such situations are absolutely critical. A change is necessary only if something simply can't continue in the same way without the church falling down. Even then, don't do it alone. Get others involved in the process of looking at the problem and creating possible solutions.

There will be some members, usually well intended, who will see the arrival of a new pastor as the perfect opportunity to make some changes. Do not be swept along by their agendas. Postpone major changes for at least a year, if not several. Even when looking at something relatively minor that seems to be innocuous, you may very well offend someone unintentionally. In the first few weeks and months of ministry, most changes are not worth the risk. It will take too long to win back someone's trust.

For example, in our church nursery, there is a sand table that generations of children have played in. The table was made decades ago, long before such tables became popular in early-education classrooms. It has been a favorite activity of the preschool set for generations. However, sand is difficult to clean up; it adheres to hair, skin, and clothes and is frequently tracked to different rooms in the church. I was aware that many child-care programs now use rice in the sand table because it is much easier to manage and keep clean. In my first week of ministry, I offered my helpful advice and mentioned how much more convenient it would be to replace the sand with rice. I was met with a friendly, but firm, "That is not how we do the sand table here."

Although changing to rice would have been more practical, churches rarely operate in the most efficient manner. The church is not to be confused with a business. It was not worth the uproar that would have resulted if I had mentioned it again. Once was enough. The sand table symbolized generations of children playing with the same toy that a dearly beloved man had fashioned years before.

Be wary of change. Keep in mind that you can win the battle but lose the war. If too many small changes are made without congregational support, members will feel overwhelmed and resentful. Then when bigger, more important changes need to be made, members will have too much difficulty trying to adapt.

One area in which to tread carefully is the order of worship. Worship is an emotionally charged topic for many churches. Everything from the order of worship to musical styles and instruments can, and does, create conflict. In one congregation, you'll find members who prefer a more traditional format, others who want a more contemporary style, and others who want it to stay exactly the same.

Understand that your presence alone is going to mean some pretty big changes for your members. You will have a different style, tone, and perspective in your sermons alone. Your prayers will have a different approach, and your face is new. You are likely to find that some people, particularly older members, get overwhelmed easily by changes, especially those in worship. They may have worshiped there for decades. Be sensitive to their needs.

Pastors must earn the right to make changes in a church. By being called to be a pastor, you have only earned the right to preach and get to know the people. Do not assume that being the new pastor gives you carte blanche to decide how the show is run. Initially the most freedom you will have is in deciding what to preach. Pray about the needs of the church at a given time, and God may lead you to preach on some of those concerns, without your using the sermon as a whip.

Above all, spend time getting to know the people and what their needs are. A wise pastor places a high priority on getting to know her or his members. Changes can come later, when the timing is right and the needs are obvious to everyone.

Resources

Loren Mead, *Critical Moment of Ministry: A Change of Pastors*. The Alban Institute, 1991.

Charles R. Swindoll, *Hand Me Another Brick: Principles of Effective Leadership*. Nelson Books, 1978.

Elmer L. Towns, *Putting an End to Worship Wars*. Broadman & Holman Publishers, 1997.

CHAPTER 3

Putting Things in Order
Organizing for Ministry

Some people are born organizers. Unfortunately, I am not one of them. My secretary, in contrast, knows if someone comes in and swipes a paper clip from her desk. Her computer discs are lined up alphabetically, and her files are immaculate. My desk, on the other hand, is a little more "lived-in."

Like it or not, pastors must learn to organize at least on a rudimentary level. Nothing looks worse than a pastor who forgets a meeting or neglects to meet a family at the hospital for a planned surgery because she or he didn't write it on the calendar. It will not be soon forgotten. Losing letters, bills, or other important documents in a paper stack also creates unnecessary havoc for treasurers, committee leaders, and ultimately you.

Organizing Your Time

Deciding how to divide up your time is a noble task and worthy of your attention. Pastors' time must be divided between personal study, sermon preparation, family life, and pastoral responsibilities. If time-management skills were an issue for you in seminary, you may want to consider doing some extra reading on this subject. There are a number of good books available, a few of which are listed in the resources at the end of this chapter.

One major way that pastoring a church differs from seminary is that, as pastor, you have much more of a free rein on your time. While there may have been many time demands in seminary, graduate school often consists primarily of attending classes and study groups and spending long hours reading and doing research. Your class schedule goes along a fairly predictable pattern as outlined on the syllabus without many surprises.

This is not true for the parish. Rarely does a week go by that a pastor does not have at least one unexpected event that demands attention. Someone will either need crisis counseling or have an unexpected hospital stay. Because of the uncertainty of a pastor's schedule, you cannot leave your schedule to chance. A certain amount of planning is essential.

There are several types of demands on your time. They include, but are not limited to:

- sermon/Bible study preparation
- counseling sessions
- church meetings
- administrative work
- other church functions
- community events/local pastors' groups

If you are not intentional about the way you spend your time, it is too easy to waste it and to neglect things that matter. You need to develop some sort of process that helps you decide which pastoral and personal responsibilities are the most important.

Establishing Your Job Description

Most pastors have a small group of members that form an oversight committee or pastor-church relations group to whom you are accountable. This group can be a valuable asset. As soon as is reasonable in your new pastorate, sit down with the committee and go over your job description, if there is one written out. If there isn't, now is a good time to begin developing one. Together, go through the job description and decide what responsibilities have the most value and that, consequently, deserve greater amounts of your time.

For example, if pastoral care is the most critical, then what percentage of time, on average, does the group want you to spend each week making pastoral calls and holding counseling sessions? Forty percent? Fifty percent? If providing an excellent worship service is critical, then how much time during the week are you expected to spend on it? Two days? One? Let the group help you set priorities for how your time is spent.

This allows the group to be a partner in your ministry. Needless to say, it is important that you stay faithful to the description that is hammered out. You can then go back in a quarter or in six months and reevaluate how it is working. If you only allotted 10 percent of your time to worship preparation, are your sermons reflecting inadequate study time? Or is too much time spent making visits, leaving office administration lacking?

You may not want to be quite that specific, but you do

need guidance on what the church's priorities are. Remember that every church is different and what was important to your last church may be irrelevant here. You may want to go through this process even if only for your own benefit.

Priorities that generally get top billing are pastoral care and planning for worship and Bible study. Large chunks of time are essential to do these things well. Committee meetings will require your attendance but often without needing much preparation, just your presence as a warm body. Community events are low on my list of priorities, although I try to attend the local pastors' monthly meetings and one community event quarterly.

Preparing a written monthly report can be very helpful. Too many church members have no idea how their pastor spends her or his time. Many members of your church will only see you on Sunday mornings. While they probably realize that you do a little more than preach on Sunday mornings, they aren't exactly sure what occupies you during the week.

Turning in a monthly report is a visual time sheet that lets board members know how your time is spent. For example, some members may have vague notions that you should call on people more often because you only visited them once in recent memory. In reality, even if you make twenty nonemergency pastoral calls a month, you may only see each family one time a year. Unless members have a clear picture of what your days and weeks look like, they may feel that they are not getting appropriate pastoral care.

No matter how you decide to spend your time, it is absolutely critical that you set aside family time. Without appropriate planning, pastors' families too often get whatever time is leftover, which is frequently too little to maintain close family ties. What kind of time you need depends on your family. For some pastors, their day off is absolute, with only emergency situations interrupting. For others, a more flexible approach is best. I take one day off during the week, usually Monday, though it varies. I also like to keep my Saturday and Sunday afternoons free, both to prepare for and then recover from Sunday morning services.

Organizing Your Office

Equal in importance to keeping your own time organized is keeping track of your office. Maintaining an organized office is absolutely necessary. Few pastors enjoy it, and some are blessed to have full-time secretaries to whom they can turn over this task. If you aren't one of them, however, this chapter is for you.

Getting started on the right foot helps. Nevertheless, it is never too late to tame the "paper tiger." Just dealing with your incoming mail appropriately is important. One of the things that amazed me in my early weeks of ministry was the incredible *volume* of mail that I received. I was on mailing lists for church supplies, civic organizations, denominational committees and interest groups, and every fund-raising company in North America.

Upon arriving at my first church, I found a file cabinet drawer full of unopened mail. Some of it was old bills and other important documents. I spent an entire afternoon just reading and sorting, trying to decide what could be tossed and what needed my attention. Being careful with your mail may seem like an inconsequential matter, but it is worth doing right.

I recommend opening your mail by the trash can, immediately weeding out any junk mail in which you have no interest.

The first few weeks are the worst because you aren't sure what is important and what isn't. Hopefully, your church will have some sort of a mailbox through which you can distribute mail to the appropriate chairperson.

Maintaining General Files

A four-drawer file cabinet used to be essential to any pastor's office. However, due to recent technological advances, most files can be kept on disc; membership records are kept on computer programs; and even personal planners are being replaced by electronic handheld devices. However, you will still need to maintain a certain number of paper files, especially for various church committee documents.

For my own files, I find it helpful to maintain twelve monthly folders. During the month, I drop in committee reports, attendance records, pastor's reports, and even sermons. When announcements about future events arrive, file them in the appropriate folder. Clean out the folders at least once a year for a relatively low-maintenance approach.

You may also want to keep folders marked "To Read" and "To File" at the front of your file drawer. When you find something you want to keep but don't want to take the time to file, throw it in one of those folders. At the end of the year, spend an hour or two weeding through these papers, and decide what is necessary to keep for church records.

If your church owns a computer, and most do, then you will want to learn as much as you can about the system as soon as you can. It will enable you to know what information is already maintained and how to access it. Many churches maintain membership, attendance, and policy information on the computer. It's worth learning. However, be mindful not to keep sensitive information about people on a disc or file that is readily accessible to other members.

Storing Important Documents

An important concern for pastors is maintaining necessary documents for the IRS. Most pastors are self-employed and consequently must keep detailed expense records, mileage sheets, and parsonage expense receipts. The IRS regularly audits pastors, and, unfortunately, ignorance of the requirements is not an adequate defense.

It is important to remember that if you receive money for moving, car allowance, parsonage allowance, professional expenses, or any other special funds, you need to be able to provide accurate records. Honoraria for weddings and funerals must be reported as well. In many cases, canceled checks do not count as adequate verification for the IRS, so save copies of registration forms, receipts, and any other documentation you might need to have on hand in case you are audited.

Because tax laws change so frequently, it isn't helpful to go into more detail here. One well-kept secret is that pastors who have been ordained (or the denominational equivalent) for twenty-four months or less can file as a Conscientious Objector and refuse to participate in the Social Security system. It would obviously be best to consult a certified financial planner for retirement and disability planning if you are considering this option.

Several good books and helpful computer programs are on the market that are specifically aimed at pastors. Again, see the list of resources below for a place to start. If you want your taxes professionally done, ask other pastors in the community which accountants they would recommend. You will want to find one who has experience dealing with pastors' special concerns, or at least one who works frequently with self-employed professionals.

Keeping Up with Correspondence

Writing letters to members is a very important task, albeit an often tedious one. Members expect to hear from their pastor during major life changes. Even though you may call to say "congratulations" on the new job, baby, or retirement, a letter is a nice, professional touch. It is another way to show members that they are cared for during special times in their lives, particularly if your limited time makes it difficult to make home visits for these events.

Members need to hear from you when great things happen in their lives. For a special anniversary, an election, or when a member's name is in the news, it adds to the occasion to have a letter from you. When babies are born, send letters to the parents, grandparents, and even great-grandparents. They love it. Your members will appreciate your thoughtfulness.

Members especially need to hear from you when tragedy touches their lives. In the death of a family member or friend, the loss of a job, or even the end of a marriage, they need to know that their church still loves them and is willing to walk with them through difficult times. When children are involved, I even send notes of condolence on the death of a family pet. Do not neglect this area of ministry—it is too important.

It is also a nice touch to send a thank-you letter to people who go the extra mile for the church. Once a year, all staff members should receive a letter thanking them for a job well done. Even the custodian likes to hear how clean the church looks on Sunday morning! Sunday school teachers, youth leaders, people who mow the lawn and replace light bulbs, are all good candidates for a thank-you note. You might also put their names in the bulletin or newsletter, although some members want to keep their good deeds low-key. Rarely are pastors criticized for showing too much pastoral care.

It can be difficult sometimes to know what to say in certain situations. Fortunately, there are several good books on the market that offer sample pastoral letters for hundreds of pastoral needs, a few of which are listed below. Topics included range from offering condolences on the loss of a job to reprimanding a staff member to tendering a pastor's resignation. While I would not recommend simply inserting a member's name in the blank, these books can be a helpful resource for ideas on what to say and how to say it. Then personalize the letter with your own insight and thoughts.

Getting and staying organized is not an easy task. However, it isn't any easier to look for lost committee reports, budget proposals, or tax documents. The extra time and energy it takes to become organized is worth it.

Resources

James D. Berkley, ed., *Leadership Handbook of Management and Administration*. Baker Book House, 1997.

Daniel D. Busby, *The Zondervan Minister's Tax and Financial Guide 1998: For 1997 Tax Returns*. Zondervan Publishing House, 1998. (This book is revised every year or two.)

ClergyTax software, based on TurboTax Software. 1998.

David J. Epstein and J. David Epstein, *Clergy Tax 1998: A Tax Preparation Manual Developed for Clergy in Cooperation with IRS Tax Officials*. Regal Books, 1997.

Franklin Gillis Jr., *It's About Time*. C.S.S. Publishing Co., 1989.

Manfred Holck Jr., *The Clergy Desk Book*. Abingdon Press, 1990.

CHAPTER 4

Being a "Home-Goin' Preacher"
Making Home and Hospital Visits

There is an old adage that says, "A home-goin' preacher makes for a church-goin' people." Is it true? All pastors have their own opinions about the reliability of the statement. Nevertheless, every pastor also has to make some visits to members' homes or hospital rooms. It is, quite simply, inevitable. The amount of visiting that will be expected of a pastor will vary from church to church. However, unless you are in a large multiple-staff church, as pastor, you will have to learn to make some visits.

Do Your Members Want to Be Visited?

Not every church wants its pastor to go visiting from family to family. It is important to understand the expectations that your members have of you regarding visitation. Start with asking your church board or whatever group supervises your ministry. Ask individuals who seem to have their fingers on the pulse of the congregation. Do members want to be visited only when they are in the hospital or sick at home? Do they want you to make calls to every family once a year, or should you visit only in emergencies?

Whom Should You Visit?

More and more families have both adults in the workplace, making it difficult to find a visitation time that is convenient for all of the members of a busy, active family. As a general rule, older homebound adults prefer pastors to visit more frequently than do young families with children.

There are a number of people that need regular visits. In general, shut-ins in nursing homes or private homes need to be visited once a month if possible, or at least every other month. If a member is in the hospital overnight or longer, a visit is usually expected. If a family is going through a difficult time, whether through personal or professional difficulties, a visit may be appreciated. New families that have visited several times are also good candidates for a pastoral visit.

Home Visits

Home visits will be your most common type of visit. If you are planning to visit a family at home, it is always appropriate to call first before you drop in. While you may assume that the elderly will be at home, even seniors in their nineties can remain very active and involved in outside activities. By calling first, you will save yourself the wasted time of going to an empty house or the awkwardness of interrupting someone's schedule.

Also, by calling first, members can prepare for your arrival. They can clean the house if they would like, or they may even want to prepare refreshments for your visit. They want to enjoy their time with you, and by being prepared, they won't have to worry about the dust on the end tables, their dentist appointment in half an hour, or anything else that would distract them from the business at hand. Being prepared also gives members an opportunity to reflect on any questions about the church, their family, or their spiritual journey that they may want to discuss with you.

Once you have called to make an appointment, make a special effort to be prompt. It is inconsiderate to be late. If a delay is unavoidable, call and let the family know how late you are running and ask if they would like to reschedule. Dress professionally. You are on the job. While your weekday clothes may be less formal than your Sunday suit, it is inappropriate to be dressed in a T-shirt, jeans, or shorts.

What happens after you arrive? Spend time getting to know this member. Often, pastors do not get to spend much private time with members unless the family is in crisis. Use the time wisely. Good introductory questions include asking how long they have lived in the area or inquiring about their families. Look around the room for clues. Ask about family photos or collections of an interesting objet d'art. Share your experiences as well. Let them get to know you.

How long do you stay? Visits under half an hour feel rushed. Stay at least thirty minutes, but not longer than an hour. You would rather leave with the family wishing you could stay longer instead of wishing you had left sooner!

Hospital Visits

Hospital visits differ in several ways from home visits. First, you do not need to make an appointment. While you might want to call the patient first to see if there is a good time to visit, visiting a hospital room without warning is not considered as rude as showing up at someone's home. All the same, be sensitive to the possibility that you may need to honor hospital visiting hours, and be considerate of the patient's schedule regarding tests, meals, and rest.

Early in your ministry, drop by the hospital and ask to see the chaplain, if there is one. See if you can get a tour, find out regulations regarding parking, signing in, and pastoral visitation. Most hospitals are appreciative of local pastors and try to work with them. As a result, pastors are often allowed in any part of the hospital except the operating room and are usually allowed to visit beyond set visiting hours. However, because each hospital is different, it is wise to take care of these details before you need to see someone.

Keep your visits with hospital patients short. Fifteen to twenty minutes is long enough, unless the patient or a family member needs to talk and asks that you stay longer. When you enter the room, knock first, especially if the door is closed. When patients are hospitalized, they are often in attire and situations that are embarrassing, so be sensitive. Honor their privacy, and do not barge in without an invitation.

What Do You Say?

Ask if this is a good time for a visit or if they would rather you come by later. Even if you do not know what is wrong with the patient, do not ask. If they want to share the information, they will. If the problem is personal in nature, they may be too embarrassed to explain. And really, how much can you say to someone who says, "I'm getting recircumcised"? Instead ask questions such as, "How are things with you?" or "What kind of day has this been for you?"

Listen sympathetically, but do not offer medical advice or share horror stories of other people you know who have suffered similar problems. If other family members are present, introduce yourself if you do not know them. Do not ignore their needs. Spend some time getting to know them and how they are doing. This is a good opportunity to pastor the patient's family members, especially if they are from out of town.

Bring a Bible, and offer a word of Scripture if it seems appropriate. It helps to have several choices selected ahead of time. If your denomination celebrates Communion, you may want to offer it at this time. Unless someone is in the dying process or requests Psalm 23, don't read it. Many people consider this passage to be a funeral Scripture.

You may want to bring along a small devotional to leave behind. Always ask if they would like to pray before you leave. Do not neglect this. I have prayed with family members beside the bed of many patients who were unconscious after surgery. One such member awoke hours later and recalled the prayer that I offered word for word.

Even if family members are not present, I do not leave the side of someone who is in a coma or unconscious without praying. We do not know what such patients are capable of understanding, and we do a disservice if we assume that they can hear nothing, just because they cannot respond. Hospitals can be frightening places, and your members desperately need you to offer a word of hope and encouragement while they are there. Don't miss the chance to do so.

When Do You Go?

If someone is having surgery, try to be there before the person is taken into surgery and plan on spending the time waiting with the family until the doctor comes out and gives the surgery report. If it is minor surgery and over forty-five miles away, then you may choose not to go, depending on the type of family support the patient has. In that case, however, I would make a point to visit them at home the day before or after the procedure.

For illnesses or tests that require an overnight stay, it is a nice courtesy to visit a member. If you are in doubt about whether the patient is up to a visit, call an immediate family member and ask for his or her opinion. Another option is to call the nurses' station in the hospital and ask what the patient's nurse would recommend.

If someone has a baby, I try to be at the hospital that day or the next one, depending on the time of delivery. Do not go during labor, unless you are specifically invited. If a dad chooses not to be in the delivery room and is going to be alone, you might offer to wait with him, but a mom who is in the throes of the birthing process may not want to share such a moment with her pastor. A visit a few hours later, however, can be a special time for new families. I have found that even unchurched family members are usually receptive to a pastor's presence and a special prayer for the new life.

Short visits are critical for new moms and babies. A new mom is probably exhausted, and if she is trying to get the hang of nursing, she may not want an audience. A visit to the home a few weeks later can be helpful as well, and it may be a good time to plan a dedication service of some kind.

At the Hour of Death

At some point in your early weeks and months of ministry, you will get a call that someone in your congregation is on her or his deathbed or has had some sort of medical emergency. If at all possible, go to the hospital or to the home of the family, wherever they have gathered. If the crisis happens right before worship or if it will take you several hours to arrive, ask an elder or other church leader to go in your place until you can get there. Your presence as soon as possible is very important.

When someone is dying or has just died, family members will probably expect you to say a prayer with and for their loved one. Often the body has not yet been removed. Do not be afraid to touch the patient's hand, even if the person has died. Different denominations have their own rituals that can be said at this time, but the most important thing you bring is your presence. Family members probably will not remember your words, but they will remember the comfort you brought to the situation.

If someone is in critical condition and may not live the night, you may need to spend several hours waiting with the family. If the person has already died, the appropriate length of time for a visit can vary. One major factor is the amount of support that family members have nearby. Offer to be helpful in practical ways, too. Do they want a prayer chain started at church? Does anyone else need to be called? Listen plenty and don't leave without praying, even if your prayer just asks God for comfort during a time of suffering that we can't even begin to comprehend.

This is a difficult time for new pastors. Don't face it alone; pray on your way to the family. Ask God to guide your words, to be with you, and to allow yourself to be open to God's ministry. God can use you as an instrument of healing and comfort.

During your visits with members, you will be exposed to some of the most private, touching, powerful, painful, and

incredibly joyous times of people's lives. Your eyes will fill
with tears as you cradle a brand-new infant, and your heart
will break for your members as they say goodbye to their
parents and spouses and children. Often, it isn't easy to be
physically present and emotionally available to your members in such times, yet it is an honor and a gift from God to
be given the invitation to be there. Do not neglect it. Your
ministry will be richer, fuller, and more blessed if you make
the effort to stand by your members as they struggle
through each new stage in their lives. It is what we as
pastors are called to do.

Resources

James E. Hightower Jr., *Caring for Folks from Birth to Death*. Broad-
    man Press, 1985.

Katie Maxwell, *Bedside Manners: A Practical Guide to Visiting the Ill*.
    Baker Book House, 1990.

CHAPTER 5

Sunday's Comin'
Planning for Preaching and Worship

On the first Sunday after his seminary graduation, Jack was preaching at his new church, a small congregation in a rural community. Over the course of several weeks, Jack had sweated bullets writing and then rewriting his sermon for that morning. He attempted to summarize all of the important doctrinal truths and theological proofs that had been so important for his spiritual development in seminary.

Finally, Sunday morning came. He delivered the sermon extremely well, then sat down, realizing with alarm that he had preached for a grand total of only twelve minutes, ending worship eighteen minutes early. And what was worse, Jack had absolutely nothing left to say for next week's message. Suddenly, preaching every Sunday all year long seemed like a daunting responsibility.

Need for Planning

Planning for worship is a difficult task. Few new pastors do it well. More often than not, pastors fresh out of seminary are still scrambling on Saturday night to finish the sermon for the next morning. In my first few months of ministry, I would get knots in my stomach on Sunday afternoons, already worried about what I was going to say next week. Living hand to mouth with your sermons is needlessly difficult and unnerving.

Larger churches have worship committees that help plan themes, but most churches do not. Generally, the pastor sets the tone and theme for worship. It is an awesome responsibility and should not be taken lightly. The most well-organized pastors plan worship months ahead of time. Planning ahead allows for the entire worship service to be centered around a theme and encourages a more reflective and methodical approach to choosing sermon themes.

Steps in Planning

The first step to take is to plan when to start planning. Some pastors like to plan at the beginning of the year. After the Christmas holidays is a good time because things tend to be slow for several weeks. Other pastors prefer to plan in the summer and work from September to August. The process of planning can take at least one or two weeks, so schedule the rest of your calendar accordingly.

Some pastors plan a year in advance, scheduling hymns, sermon titles, Scripture passages, and Bible study topics all at once. They take a calendar and fill in special holidays, services, guest speakers, and other notable events. This method, although time consuming, has its merits and, once done, saves an incredible amount of time during the year.

For many pastors, scheduling once a quarter is more realistic because, naturally, a quarter's worth of services can be done within a more manageable time frame. Hymns and special music may also be chosen in advance to complement the sermon themes. When pastors are scheduling themes quarterly, they can coordinate with the Sunday school themes. This works well when all the classes use the same publisher and when each age-group studies the same topic. Related themes can be a helpful reinforcement for both worship and Sunday school, allowing members the opportunity to reflect on and discuss the topics.

If in no other part of your ministry, planning your sermons is crucial. There is nothing worse than staring at a blank computer screen late Saturday night in a frenzied attempt to write a sermon. To avoid hours of panic and Saturday-night pacing, your schedule of sermons must be well planned. This is not a guarantee against last-minute fumbling, but it will go a long way towards prevention.

Begin with Prayer

Pray for the help of the Holy Spirit as you plan your services. The Holy Spirit can be as active in planning sermons well in advance as in planning week by week. Seek God's guidance about what God's church in that place needs to hear. Are there areas of growth that God is pointing out to you? Spend some time brainstorming and seeking God's will for your messages.

You can also ask others to intercede for you. Is there a prayer group or committee that oversees worship? Let them know of your planning sessions and seek their prayer support as well. Members will not mind praying for their pastor's planning, though they may not have been invited to do so before.

Focus on Needs

The longer you are in the pastorate, the better you will know your members. Because you are counseling them, in your office and at hospital bedsides, you know the needs of your congregation. During one difficult time in the life of my church, three people under the age of forty were diagnosed with serious brain tumors, two of whom later died. During that time in the life of the congregation, the church needed to deal with difficult issues such as "why bad things happen to good people" and questions about Christ's sufficiency.

One pastor says that he can safely assume that six out of ten people sitting in the pews are struggling with some kind of heartache, including many of which we are not aware. Be sensitive. One of the worst accusations against the twentieth-century church is that we are not relevant and do not attempt to meet our own people's needs. Life events of your members must affect the tone and topic of your sermons.

Don't feel as though you have to do the brainstorming entirely on your own. Ask a few members you trust about what current needs are in the congregation and in the community. Even if you cannot pinpoint members affected by particular community events, their friends, families, and co-workers can. Look through your church directory, and make notes about some of the families' current struggles. Are the needs physical, financial, emotional? How can God use the sermon time to help meet those needs?

Choose a Theme

Some pastors prefer to vary their topics from week to week. That is a personal choice. I have found that congregations often prefer to stay with one particular topic for a month or more. First, they know what to expect and come prepared, if not in their own study, then in their thought processes. Second, analyzing a topic or Scripture passage can be done more thoroughly over several weeks than in half an hour. Some pastors will use the Scripture for Sunday morning as the topic for midweek Bible studies to engage both themselves and the people more thoroughly in the text.

Planning your sermons on quarterly or monthly themes helps ensure that your sermons are balanced. That is, you may not realize that you preach only on the death and resurrection of Christ but never address Christ's parables or God's faithfulness throughout the Old Testament. Planning helps avoid needless repetition in your preaching and encourages deeper personal study and greater spiritual growth for your members. Strive for balance in your choice of topics. Try alternating between topical studies and Scripture dissection. If you spend one month discussing the life of King David, then use the next for outlining prayer.

Spend some time thinking of as many themes as you can. Possible themes include:

- The Parables
- The Kingdom of God
- The Ten Commandments
- The Church
- The Beatitudes
- The Fruits of the Spirit
- Knowing God
- Growing in Christ
- Touched by Jesus
- Asking God the Tough Questions

You may also choose to focus on a certain book of the Bible or to study a group of biblical characters such as the prophets, judges, or apostles.

Add Holidays and Other Special Observances

Next, schedule the Sundays on which you'll present your series and what the topics will be. Be aware of holidays and church seasons as you plan. Include annual events such as Youth Sunday, Women's Day, etc. Understand that current events may force you to adapt later. When the Federal Building in Oklahoma City was bombed, I did a radical change in the sermon topic for that Sunday. During the military crisis with Iraq, my focus also changed.

Be flexible when situations demand attention. When members' entire world-views are shattered by a tragedy or unexpected local news, it is negligent to ignore the feelings and fears of your congregation. It is important for members to know and experience that their church is as relevant as their morning newspaper. They need to be reminded that God is still present and still active in human affairs.

Don't Keep It to Yourself

Share your calendar with anyone else who would be helped by such information. This could include the music or choir director, worship leader, or maybe just the secretary. Advance planning allows other worship elements to be planned that may add greater impact, such as dramatic or musical presentations. Also, when sermons are planned in advance, hymns can be selected that will be more meaningful.

Sermon Preparation

Sermon preparation is very different for each pastor. There are few hard-and-fast rules regarding how much time you need to prepare and how preparation should be done. In seminary, I was taught that a pastor should spend one hour of preparation time for each minute of preaching every single week. However, it did not take long to discover that the rule was perhaps an unrealistic expectation for pastors with many other important responsibilities.

A recent survey of American pastors found that they spent anywhere from four to twenty hours per week on sermon preparation. It is, for all of us, a time-consuming task. A pastor who preaches weekly for forty years will spend over 40,000 hours in sermon preparation. No matter how much time you spend, use it well.

Where do you begin? Begin with prayer for God's leading. Read the Scripture passage you have chosen several times and in several different versions. If you are able, reading it in the original language is helpful but not necessary. Make a careful study of the biblical passage first.

Jot down notes. Find the most important information in the text and list it. Then add peripheral details. Do not go to a commentary too soon, or you will not engage the text carefully enough. Look for what speaks to you. What is God's message here? How does this text speak to the members of your congregation?

One of the things that is most important when preparing your sermon is to identify the thesis—the main point that you want to emphasize. Can folks walk away explaining your sermon in one short sentence? No sermon is ready for preaching unless the pastor can express its theme in a brief, clear statement. Developing that one sentence may be the most difficult part of the sermon, but it will also be the most fruitful. Only once you have established a concise statement of your theme do you look for secondary points.

Everything else in the sermon needs to go back to that original thesis. More than once, I have been in the middle of writing a sermon and realized that either I did not have a point or I had left it behind along the way. The rest of the sermon structure can vary in a hundred ways, but establishing your thesis is the most important place to begin.

Having done that, go on to your collection of commentaries and other homiletical resources. Sermon resources are more widely available now than ever before. Every Christian bookstore has at least one shelf of pastor's notes, outlines, and even complete sermons. In fact, complete sermons from a variety of pastors are also available in monthly newsletters as well as on CD-ROM, so you only have to print out the sermon you want for the week.

Everyone has a different perspective on using others' sermon notes and texts. Individual pastors must work out for themselves how much of others' materials they are willing to use in the sermon preparation process. While some disparage the use of any outside resources, most pastors find a good balance that works. The primary concern is not to substitute weaker material or illustrations to cover up a lack of disciplined research and reading on our part. There is no substitute for searching out God's word to your people.

There are several drawbacks to using a great deal of materials authored by other people. First, although the writer may have great ideas, she or he may not sound like you. Consequently, the material may not feel authentic to others. Second, it is more difficult to fit someone else's thoughts into what is happening in your congregation and in your members' lives. As well, too much reliance on others will stifle your own personal and spiritual growth.

Perhaps the most important thing to keep in mind in preparing your sermon is to give it over to God. Remember who owns it. Ask God to prepare the hearts of the listeners so that they might grow in their relationships with Christ. Writing a sermon is often difficult. It is also what God has called you to do. The process takes a great deal of time and energy, but it is also richly satisfying to struggle with a text, wrestle with it, and bring forward new insights that are deeply personal. Pastors do not come away from the process unchanged. Hopefully, neither do our members. And if God has called you to preach, then God has given you what you need to do the job.

Resources

David Buttrick, *Preaching Jesus Christ*. Fortress Press, 1988.

Bryan Chapell, *Using Illustrations to Preach with Power*. Zondervan, 1992.

Samuel DeWitt Proctor, *"How Shall They Hear?": Effective Preaching for Vital Faith*. Judson Press, 1992.

Bruce Mawhinney, *Preaching with Freshness*. Kregel Publications, 1997. Abingdon Press, 1980.

CHAPTER 6

Behind Closed Doors
Keys to Effective Counseling

I will never forget the first time someone came in for counseling at the first church I pastored. A middle-aged woman stood in the doorway of the church office where I was talking with my secretary. We chatted briefly for a few minutes, and then I realized that she might want something. I asked if she needed to talk to me, and when she said yes, at first I was surprised. Then panic set in.

For the first few minutes of our time together, I wondered, "What if I have no idea what to say? What if I have to look her in the face and tell her I do not have any idea what to do? I'm not even unpacked yet!" Terrified by the idea of having to load everything back into the moving van, I quickly prayed and was then able to listen to the woman's needs and remembered some tools that could be helpful.

About half the people who seek professional counseling go to a pastor before they will go anywhere else for assistance. Pastors are frequently sought as counselors because they are known and trusted and can offer a spiritual perspective for their members' situation. While you may have few sessions in the early months, as members get to know you, the visits will become more frequent.

No Easy Answers

The most important thing to do is to listen. Listening closely and carefully to someone's pain is a rare gift that you can offer that person. There are many members of your church who do not have someone willing to sit and listen. Often, when people need an opportunity to talk about problematic situations and their feelings about them, just having a sounding board helps. Listening without interruption and maintaining eye contact are important.

Respond with statements that help the person share: "I can't imagine how you felt." "I don't know how I would handle that." "How have you coped so far?" These are all nonjudgmental statements that give permission for the person to continue.

Have a comfortable chair or couch for members to sit in. An upholstered chair is much more comfortable than a stiff-backed wooden one or metal folding chair. Also, don't forget to keep a box of tissues next to your chair. It seems like a minor thing, but it makes a difference. If someone has to get up and go in search of a tissue, the counseling process is significantly disrupted.

One of the biggest misconceptions about counseling is that the counselor has to give advice. However, if we give advice, then we become responsible for the outcome. As a general rule, people who come in to see us already know the answers they seek. They just need the freedom to explore possible solutions and a safe environment in which to find their own way.

Nevertheless, there will be times when a pastor will need to confront members about their behavior. If a member is having an adulterous relationship, for example, then the pastor can hold up a higher standard and call the member to uphold it. However, just calling a behavior a sin and telling the person to stop is rarely effective. Pastors can help parishioners try to understand why they are engaging in self-destructive behaviors.

Maintain Confidentiality

One of the most important things that people will want to know about their pastor is that you can be trusted. They need to know that what they tell you will not be shared with anyone else. You've heard that loose lips sink ships; they also sink careers, reputations, and friendships. It cannot be said too strongly that confidentiality is absolutely critical to building and keeping a strong relationship between you and your church family.

Information that is shared with you cannot be shared with anyone else, even the member's family. Although you may want to encourage the person to share information with her or his spouse, the decision is not yours to make. Confidentiality also extends to prohibiting you from telling members of your own family, particularly your spouse. It is not only professionally unethical to reveal information shared in confidence; it is unfair to "unload" on your partner about particular counseling situations.

Several lawsuits have been won by members against pastors who have not maintained confidentiality. Counseling files kept in unlocked offices or information shared with other members can create a legal nightmare and damaged relationships with members. These confidential files are best left in a locked file cabinet, in your office at the church or at home. If you don't have a secure cabinet, then at least lock your office door when you are not there.

There are a few exceptions to the overall principle of confidentiality. For example, if a child is being abused in any way, including physical, sexual, or emotional abuse or neglect, the law requires you to intervene with outside assistance. While laws vary from state to state, you have a moral responsibility to become involved. Generally, the local social services department needs to become involved. Calling the local school counselor is a good place to start because that office will know who should be called.

Additionally, if someone is seriously planning to hurt himself or herself or someone else, then again you have a legal and moral obligation to intervene. But even then I advise telling the person, "Because I care about you and I don't want you to be hurt, I need to call someone to help you. Can I take you to the hospital, or would you like someone else to come and take you?" When you break a confidence, do so only if it is unavoidable for the member's safety and well-being, and tell the person why.

Know Your Limits

It is critical to know your limits in counseling. There are some problems that many pastors are simply not equipped to handle. Even an excellent seminary education cannot offer the amount and type of training in mental-health counseling that some of your members will need. Be aware of what your limitations are in the counseling field.

For example, there are many types of mental illness that

respond well to medication or a specific type of therapy. A pastor who tries to treat someone who is clinically depressed or schizophrenic does a disservice to the member. Similarly, people with alcohol and drug addictions or eating disorders are best served by a trained professional.

You need to have a healthy balance between working with members yourself and referring them to outside sources of help. Be aware that members may have to go to specialists who have more training in particular areas, and don't be afraid to refer. However, if there is a need, feel free to continue counseling with your members and work on their spiritual issues.

Some pastors prefer to refer members to outside services if a problem cannot be solved in three sessions. I would recommend that, rather than imposing strict time guidelines, you should be flexible and look for signs of progress. It can be helpful to ask members what they would like to happen in your time together. Allow them to take responsibility for and ownership of their counseling and not remain passive participants.

For example, with one couple I was seeing for marriage counseling, we set goals for each session. Their long-term goal was to learn how to argue in a healthy way. The first goal we set was, when they got angry with each other, they could not hit, throw things at each other, or storm out of the house. It took a few weeks to accomplish it, but they did.

It took months of work before they got to the point where they could calmly have a disagreement and resolve it, but because tangible progress was being made, it worked well to meet together over an extended period of time. However, we met more frequently in the beginning and began tapering off the visits. For a member with severe problems, I recommend that you meet weekly and then gradually increase the length of time between sessions.

Know Community Resources

Once you have settled in, it is critical to learn what your community offers in terms of mental health resources. It would be unfortunate to have someone call you after normal office hours with a fairly immediate need and not know where to turn. Most cities have a variety of agencies, hospitals, counseling centers, and chemical dependency programs with an incredible range of services offered and prices charged.

Members of your church may be in the mental health field or in the medical community and can be a good resource. Also, don't forget to ask around at your local community pastors' gathering. Ask what is available in the area and to whom they recommend their members. Then spend some time calling local mental health agencies and learn about what services they have to offer. Some questions to consider are:

- What services are offered? (e.g., in-patient, out-patient, counseling services)
- What specialties are offered? (e.g., eating disorders, chemical abuse, sexual abuse)
- Who are the primary clients served? (e.g., children, adults, teenagers, women)
- What are the qualifications of the counseling staff?
- What are the operating hours?
- Are there emergency assessments and in-takes available?
- What are the payment options? (e.g., sliding scale, health insurance, out of pocket)

• What is the methodological approach? (You may want to refer someone only to a Christian counselor.)

Special Circumstances

Some types of counseling may occur frequently, such as marriage counseling. Others you hope you never have to encounter. Dealing with abused children is one, and people in severe crisis is another. Nevertheless, you will be grateful later if you prepare yourself for every contingency.

Children and Teenagers

Some pastors are afraid to work with children or teenagers. Be flexible and look at each case individually. If a child is acting out after a tragedy, spending some time with the child might be helpful. If a child is having behavior problems in school without any trigger events, you might recommend that parents ask the school's psychological testing office to have the child tested for a learning disability.

Often, the first few meetings with a child or teen focus on building a relationship. I might give a young child a marker and notepad to draw on while we talk or offer the basket of puzzles I keep by the couch. With teens, spend time talking about relatively inconsequential things like movies or high school sports. Feel free to ask why they're there, especially if a parent has initiated the session. "Why do you think your mom wanted you to talk with me?" Allow the child to participate in the process.

Particularly with teenagers, maintaining confidentiality is important. Teens and older children may test you by sharing something minor one week and waiting to see if you tell their parents before sharing something major. Honor their trust, even if they admit to an undesirable behavior like premarital sex. Let them know that what they tell you stays with you, even if their parents are the ones who brought them there. Discuss this understanding with the parents before you begin seeing their children.

Marriage Counseling

Marriage is the most common reason that members of your congregation will come to see you. You may require an engaged couple to meet with you for premarital counseling before the wedding, while other couples may need help in a marriage that is older than you are. While every marriage and its difficulties are unique, you will need to be competent in dealing with couples in crisis.

Often, one member of the couple will want to talk with you more than the other. In some relationships, one partner may dominate conversations more than the other. It can be helpful to meet for individual sessions with one spouse and then the other as a part of the counseling process. Issues may arise there that can be brought to light when meeting together.

More and more counselors are using "genograms" when working with couples. Genograms are a fairly easy method of helping couples trace their family roots back for several generations. The focus is on what each spouse has brought to the marriage from her or his family of origin. The approach is simple. Ask each spouse about his or her family of origin. While each person talks, sketch out a diagram of the family structure on a notepad. What do the family trees look like? Are there siblings, blended families, divorces, or unusual deaths? What are the families' occupations, ages, marital status, health, and number of children? Once you have the family history outlined, look for areas of concern.

For example, adult children of alcoholics bring something different to their marriages than those who grew up in a close-knit family environment. Styles of arguing, disciplining children, and making decisions are a few areas that may be affected. Frequently, the discussions shed new light on both spouses' behaviors and open the door for more tolerance and the potential for change. You might read more about this subject as a method for approaching marriage counseling. See the list of resources below for a place to start.

Crisis Intervention

Inevitably, in the middle of the night a member of your church will call you and say that you need to come over right away because someone is going to commit suicide or hurt someone else. Pastors sometimes overestimate their abilities in such situations.

Simply put, there is no need to be a hero. What is needed is a professional who is trained to act in crisis situations. Let the person know that you will be there after the police arrive. Hang up; then call the police. Clearly describe the situation, the address, and any other helpful information. Then, allow enough time for the police to arrive before you do. Allow the police to take the lead and offer to be of assistance.

What Else Should You Do?

Some pastors keep a well-stocked library of helpful books that they loan to members. (See Resources below.) This is a good way to help your members, especially because of the relatively short time-frame that you have available to work with members. Other pastors find it helpful to ask parishioners who come for counseling to journal for several weeks about their experiences.

Remember that above all, you are a spiritual counselor. You bring something to the relationship that many other counselors do not. Your primary responsibility is to help people in their relationships with God. Ask each person about her or his Christian walk and how it affects the current struggle.

Don't neglect prayer. Pray with people who come in to talk with you. Even if the problem is not a spiritual one, and many aren't, it is still a good time to bring them closer to God. Ask if it's all right to pray with them, and then you might want to ask what you should pray for.

People from within your congregation and the community at large will come through your doors with an incredible array of problems ranging from marital difficulties to guilt and sin. At times, you may feel overwhelmed. Pray for those who come for counseling before they arrive and after they leave. Seek God's wisdom for your time together.

Resources

Andrew D. Lester, *Hope in Pastoral Care and Counseling*. Westminster John Knox Press, 1995.

Andrew D. Lester, *Pastoral Care with Children in Crisis*. Westminster John Knox Press, 1985.

Michael J. McManus, *Marriage Savers: Helping Your Friends and Family Avoid Divorce (revised edition)*. Zondervan Publishing House, 1994. (Also video series)

Michael J. McManus, *Insuring Marriage: 25 Proven Ways to Prevent Divorce*. Zondervan Publishing House, 1996.

Marshall Shelley, *Helping Those Who Don't Want Help (Leadership Library, Vol. 7)*. Word Books, 1986.

J. C. Wynn, *Family Therapy in Pastoral Care*. HarperSanFrancisco, 1982.

CHAPTER 7

We Are Gathered Here Today
Weddings, Funerals, and Baptisms

Presiding over weddings and funerals allows pastors to participate in some of the most personal and intimate times in people's lives. Saying good-bye to a loved one or making a lifelong commitment in front of family and friends is an incredibly important event for your members. It is an honor to be involved in people's lives in this way, and the occasions need to be treated as such.

Both weddings and funerals are rare opportunities for you to minister to people who might never be seen again inside the church walls and for the congregation to welcome new guests. Therefore, both wedding and funeral services ought to be an accurate reflection of how the body of Christ in your local church comes together in worship.

Weddings

Every pastor has an array of stories about mishaps and human foibles when it comes to wedding services. In every wedding I perform, at least one thing goes wrong.

However, some mistakes are the fault of the minister and can be avoided. For example, one pastor called a man named Robert "Sam" during the entire ceremony, not hearing the whispered corrections by the bride and groom. Guests left the ceremony wondering if the two were legally married.

Another new pastor realized the morning of the wedding that he had not gotten certified with the clerk of the court in the city. Consequently, he was not legally able to perform the two-hundred-guest wedding ceremony planned for later that afternoon. In a panic, he had to locate a pastor in a neighboring community that was both certified and available. Finally he found one who agreed to assist in the service and sign the marriage certificate.

Planning

Weddings are more enjoyable to plan than funerals, but they are much more complicated and time consuming. The occasion usually involves many more people, including attendants, musicians, photographers, florists, and family members. And to make things worse, all of these people usually know *exactly* how the wedding should be done.

If you are fortunate, your church will have a booklet of some sort that outlines appropriate guidelines for the service, music, decorations, and use of the facilities. If not, it is worth the time to develop one so you don't have to reinvent the wheel each time you meet with a new couple. Generally, you should meet with the couple early to get the date set for the church calendar and to go over your requirements for premarital counseling.

Counseling the Couple

While over 90 percent of pastors believe in the efficacy of premarital counseling, only about one-third actually require it. Tragically, couples married in the church are no more likely to stay married than those who were married in civil ceremonies. With divorce rates skyrocketing, more and more pastors are requiring some preparation for an engaged couple.

In recent years, a divorce-prevention movement has swept across the country. This movement has led denominations and communities to band together in an effort to avoid the economic and social devastation that divorce brings. As such, a number of excellent methods and resources are available for pastors to help couples whom they wed to avoid a split.

It is wise to be aware of what resources are available before the pastor is approached by a couple. New pastors need to know what kind of counseling is needed or what kind of preparation they themselves will require. The resources at the end of this chapter and the previous one may be helpful in this. Having to scramble to find appropriate materials is both time consuming and frustrating.

Besides using a variety of videos, books, and study guides that are on the market, a number of pastors use a questionnaire approach, such as Prepare/Enrich®, that can fairly accurately predict whether or not a marriage will succeed. If nothing else, the method allows a couple to look at potential problems before they tie the knot. Some churches are having success with appointing a mentor couple to work with an engaged couple before the wedding and for up to one year afterwards.

The Service

The pastor is expected to be the authority on everything that is remotely connected with a wedding. You will appreciate having a book or two on hand, like those listed below under Resources, that deal with procedures and etiquette for a variety of weddings. Many denominations have their own manuals or books offering a fixed ritual for each service. Most pastors without denominational rituals move toward having a fixed service that they use for every marriage ceremony. Whatever source you use, give a copy of the book or manual to the bride and groom so it can be discussed well in advance.

Memorizing the marriage service is an admirable task. However, for the first several weddings, keep your book of ritual, or the equivalent, with you during the service. Many pastors have thought they had the wedding service memorized only to go blank during the ceremony. Not surprisingly, a quick run to your office in the middle of a ceremony will not endear you to your parishioners.

Some couples prefer to recite their own vows. Think about what your approach will be. I prefer a couple to use the traditional format but am flexible if couples choose to express the meaning of this marriage in a different, more personal way. However, I require that the vows be written out and discussed in a counseling session beforehand.

Weddings rarely go as planned. Grooms pass out, ring bearers lose rings, and mothers of the bride lose perspective. You may be one of the few sane voices in the throng. While maintaining control of the service is a formidable task at times, you can remind the couple that what matters is the marriage and the memories, not the perfection of a well-executed performance.

Funerals

Funerals are a difficult part of pastoral life. Sometimes you will be called upon to perform funerals for faithful members who lived a long life in the Lord and died peacefully in their sleep. Other times you will be called upon to perform funerals for children, for mothers who died too soon, for victims of violent crime or suicide, and for people about whom it is difficult to say a kind word. Very few new pastors enjoy performing funerals. Nevertheless, officiating a funeral is an important task. Offering a word of hope and comfort to those who are grieving is what ministry is about.

Too many funerals never even mention the deceased person's name. Make the funeral personal. In addition to her or his faith, what else characterized the person who has died? Telling a person's story is incredibly important to those left behind; that story deserves to be told well.

The Funeral Home

You will probably be expected to attend, at least for a short visit, the viewing or visitation the day before the funeral service. Appropriate dress is generally a dark suit. Twenty minutes is usually enough time, unless the crowd is large and many of your members are present. Staying longer is also appropriate when there is very little family support. Be sure to take time to speak to all members of the family. What you say doesn't mean nearly as much as your being there. They will remember your presence long after they forget your words.

Ask for the director of the funeral home while you are at the viewing and introduce yourself. He or she will probably have a clergy record that contains important information about the deceased. Review the order of worship and make any other arrangements. Generally, the family pays the funeral home, and the director or a representative will give you a check on the day of the funeral.

Most funeral homes are excellent to work with. Generally,

they should call you after they have met with the family and tell you when the services have been planned. Here is one occasion when your schedule simply doesn't matter. You are expected to lay aside other responsibilities to accommodate this tragedy. (A potential exception may be a conflict with family vacation; that circumstance will require a difficult personal decision.)

You are expected to escort the body from funeral home to hearse and from hearse to graveside. If there is a graveside service, you will probably ride with the body. Walk by the head of the casket. If you don't know which end that is, ask the funeral director for help.

The Service

In preparation for delivering the eulogy, meet with family members before the funeral and ask them to share their memories of the deceased with you. Ask to see photo albums if any are available. Use the time at the funeral home to talk to other family members or close friends. Most will welcome the opportunity to share. Invite each family member to tell you what was special about this person. Include children in this time together, if they are old enough.

Try to discover what the person's life was like. What did she do? What gave him joy? Did she love to garden? How did he and his wife meet? What did she say when she saw her baby for the first time? Did he always wear bright-colored clothes in patterns that never matched? What was the driving force in her life?

Take some time and gather your thoughts. Weave the memories together. Attempt to tell the story in a way that is honorable and fair. Don't make someone a saint; the family knows better. Acknowledging imperfections is all right. Be real and authentic rather than leaving family members feeling that you weren't honest.

Avoid preaching someone into heaven or hell. What you have to say about the matter isn't going to make much of a difference at this point. Also, while theological perspectives will direct your service, stay away from trite clichés like "The Lord took this person because God needed another flower in heaven's garden" or "because the angels wanted a baby to rock." Such expressions ring hollow in the midst of grief, and they do nothing to help people reconnect with God.

Above all, do not tell people how they ought to feel. Be honest. Acknowledge that "Even when someone has suffered as much or as long as this person did, the selfish part of us wanted to hold on." Or when there has been a tragedy, don't hesitate to admit, "It's hard to understand why things like this happen, and we feel angry at God because the Lord didn't stop it from happening." We turn people away from God when we tell them that they should not be sad because their loved ones are with God. We don't know how people ought to feel. What we do know is that God loves them no matter what they're feeling. So, do not be scared away by raw pain and grief. Give people permission to be honest with God. Allow people to own their feelings.

And then offer grace. Offer hope. Bring forward the promise of eternal life. Remind those present about God's love that carries us through things we don't even understand because divine love is strong enough to withstand all of our emotions, even anger and agony.

At the end of the service, walk to the family and extend a hand and a kind word to each friend and family member on the front row. Again, your words do not have to be original. "God bless you" is fine. Stand near the casket until the family has left.

If memorials are sent to the church, acknowledge each gift with a thank-you note, explaining how the gift will be used. Within a few weeks, send a note with a list of all the contributors to the person's family. They will want to send their own cards as well.

By some odd quirk of human nature, I cry at funerals—all of them, even if I have never met the deceased. I find that my voice sometimes cracks with emotion as I lay to rest a fellow sojourner. A display of emotion is fine as long as it is genuine and appropriate. Loud, unrestrained weeping, however, is not.

Details, Details

Every pastor needs to decide whether or not to accept payment for performing weddings and funerals. It is a good idea to ask a member of your board what pastors at that church have traditionally done. Some churches have set fees for weddings, and funeral homes often dictate the fee for funerals. Some pastors refuse any form of payment for either ceremony; others will accept the money graciously and then donate it to a scholarship or memorial committee. If you do choose to redirect the money, a note to the family expressing thanks and explaining your intention is appreciated. Other pastors accept payment as a supplement to rather low pastoral salaries.

Each denomination has its own traditions regarding appropriate pastoral clothing for weddings and funerals. Many pastors wear a dark suit with a white or light-colored shirt. In some churches, a clerical robe or shirt with a collar is more appropriate. A good rule of thumb is that it is better to be dressed more professionally and conservatively than too casually.

Baby Dedications and Baptisms

Dedicating or baptizing an infant is a special time in the life of the church. Look for ways to make it special for everyone involved. Avoid, if possible, having a private service for family members. Most denominations dedicate or baptize infants with the theological understanding that an important part of the ceremony is the commitment that the church family is making to the baby and its family. The congregation is committing to provide good role models, to offer Sunday school classes, and to love the infant and help it grow.

Spend time with the family planning the service. Discuss what kind of commitment they are making during this ceremony. Talk with the parents about what this occasion means to them. Is there something important to them that they would like to include? For example, a white rose was dipped in the water when my husband was baptized, and he wanted the same thing for our daughter's dedication.

Make the ceremony special. I walk the infant up and down the center aisle of the church (if it is content), allowing everyone to meet the baby. I tell the congregation that in a few minutes I am going to ask them to make a commitment to this child and its family, and I want them to get a good look at the one to whom they will make that promise.

Some churches give the parents something as a symbolic reminder of the day, such as a rose or a certificate. Some plan a fellowship dinner or reception following the service so the whole church has an opportunity to celebrate with the family afterwards. Making families feel accepted and cherished is an important ministry.

Resources

WEDDINGS

Paul E. Engle, ed., *Baker's Wedding Handbook*. Baker Book House, 1994.

Jim Henry, *The Pastor's Wedding Manual*. Broadman & Holman Publishers, 1985.

Life Innovations, Inc. 1-800-331-1661. This organization offers premarital and marriage counseling.

The Sourcebook of Weddings. Communications Resources, Inc.

FUNERALS

Paul E. Engle, ed., *Baker's Funeral Handbook: Resources for Pastors*. Baker Book House, 1996.

Daniel S. Lloyd, *Leading Today's Funeral: A Pastoral Guide for Improving Bereavement Ministry*. Baker Book House, 1997.

The Sourcebook of Funerals. Communications Resources, Inc.

CHAPTER 8

Thriving in a Fish Bowl
Balancing Your Family Life

During my first month as senior pastor in a midsize city, I received a call from a member who mentioned I had been seen at a local discount store. Someone from the church had seen me shopping, and upon arriving at home, that member called another member and mentioned to her where I had been and what I had purchased. While buying toilet paper and toothpaste was a fairly innocuous event, it was a good reminder that pastors often do not know who is watching or when.

"Living in a fish bowl" is a description that most pastoral families have learned to accept, particularly if they live in a church-owned parsonage. Like it or not, church members and their friends and families are watching you and your family closely. This is usually done in friendly interest. The smaller the city, the higher the interest in a pastor's life outside the church walls.

Church members may watch what groceries you buy, how

you keep up your yard, and how your children behave and dress. More alarming is that some pastors have had members listen in on phone conversations and go through their medicine cabinets and trash cans. Balancing your church family's need to know about your life and your own family's need to have one can be tricky.

One of the most common regrets that older pastors have is that they did not spend enough time with their families. Too often, a pastor's spouse and children are sacrificed on the altar of the pastor's work schedule. However, this is not inevitable. Your family has some needs that are absolutely critical.

Your Family's Needs

Your Presence

First, your family needs you—physically and emotionally. Your spouse needs you as a friend, companion, lover, and ally. She or he needs to talk about the pressures in her or his life. Your children need you desperately as a parent. They need to depend on and spend time with *both* of their parents.

One of the advantages of being a pastor is that you often have a flexible schedule. Generally, you can plan a day off for chaperoning field trips or attending other special events. Yes, emergencies do occur during the most inopportune times, sometimes on the way out the door for a family event. But pastors can help set limits to minimize those times.

In my church, everyone understands that Mondays are my day off. As a rule, people do not call my house on that day unless there is an emergency. You may choose not to answer the telephone on your day off, allowing the answering machine to screen messages. If the need is urgent, you can return the call immediately. If not, call back the next day.

The same rule holds true for dinnertime. The evening meal is an important time for your family. Too often, pastors become slaves to the ringing of the phone and feel as if they must jump to answer it when it beckons. Your family deserves better. A good-quality answering machine is worth the investment.

Some pastors are connected continuously to cellular phones, beepers, and e-mail. I am not one of them. While I recognize the helpfulness of such technology in being available to anyone, at any time, anywhere, only a rare emergency necessitates such availability. Pastors and their families need to be able to get away for a few hours without being electronically wired to the church.

A Place to Call Home

Besides needing your time and energy, your family needs a home that "belongs" to them. Many churches are moving away from church-owned homes for pastors and giving them living allowances instead. But, unlike almost any other professionals, many pastors have to live in homes that they did not choose, decorate, or sometimes even furnish. If a pastor wants to redecorate, an act of Congress may be required to change the color of a carpet that was memorialized to Great-aunt Mildred thirty years ago when orange shag was popular. To complicate matters, parsonages are often only steps away from the pastor's place of employment, and too often seemingly dozens of "employers" have keys to the parsonage doors.

Clearly, living in a parsonage can be difficult, and you may need to think of ways to make your family feel comfortable there. New paint, curtains, or other decorating items may help them feel more at home in the house. Installing new locks on the door will alleviate worries about members entering without invitation. Understand, however, that pastoral families often have to entertain unannounced company with little or no notice. Unexpected guests are simply a fact of church life. Because of this, I recommend keeping one room of the house, such as the living room, presentable and ready for company. That can minimize stress when members do drop in unexpectedly.

Part of your family's need for a home of their own is a need for privacy. That need is not just geographic; they need their privacy in the psychological sense as well. Many times using your family in sermon illustrations can be very effective. However, some family members do not want to be mentioned from the pulpit or have certain stories from their lives made public. If you have a particular story you would like to share, ask your family if you can use it in a sermon. If they do not give permission, honor the refusal. I have shared a story or two that my husband would have preferred to remain private, and I have regretted doing so.

Relationships within the Church

Pastoral families need to feel connected to the church family. Family members need to be able to participate at whatever level of activity is appropriate for their age, interests, and abilities. While each family differs on its requirements for attending Sunday school, youth group, and church, it is an unfair expectation for young people to be forced to participate in an activity that lacks enjoyment simply because of their parent's job. Consider if just church and Sunday school attendance is enough, if that is the only involvement your child, particularly a teenager, wants. Work at being sensitive to your children's needs as well.

In the same way, a pastor's spouse needs to be able to enjoy fellowship in the church. Most clergy spouses have felt the frustration of being expected to do a church activity because they are married to the pastor. For many years, the pastor's wife was supposed to play the piano, sing in the choir, teach Sunday school, and participate in, if not lead, the women's ministry. A pastor's spouse often faces the same difficulties in terms of making friendships as the pastor, especially if he or she does not work outside the home. Marriage to a pastor can be a lonely life, and a spouse should be free to look outside the congregation for friendships.

Relationships outside the Church

In some respects, clergy husbands have an advantage over clergy wives because there are fewer traditional expectations placed on them. They are breaking new ground, so they are better able to find their own activities, ones that interest them. Nevertheless, they are still expected to maintain a high level of involvement regardless of outside responsibilities.

Inevitably, there will be times in your ministry when your church will be a painful place to be. Members can be hurtful, especially if they are in pain themselves. While pastors may understand this, spouses and children can be particularly hurt if an attack is directed toward them. For this reason if no other, your entire family needs a life outside the church walls. Every member of your family needs activities and interests that go beyond congregational events.

As pastor, you will appreciate being involved in other activities that you are not directly responsible for running. That in itself is freeing. Additionally, your family will like being with people who don't think of them only as the pastor's spouse and kids but who know and love them for themselves. Being involved with other people in different activities can be a lifesaver for everyone.

Financial Security

While the median pastor's salary is $32,000 a year, very few new pastors begin at a first church making that much money. No matter what your family income is, you will probably need extra help stretching your budget sometimes. This may be particularly true if one spouse stays at home with the children. Your family's financial needs need to be secured.

While you will have to become an expert on stretching your dollar, you have probably already learned the fine art of living in poverty while in seminary. A little creativity and excellent resources can be helpful here, but you will also need to look carefully at savings, investments, and retirement planning.

Many young pastors feel that they make too little to save or invest, but you should get started on the right foot. Seek the assistance of a certified financial counselor, who usually offers a free consultation. The information an expert provides can be valuable, particularly if you want to save for a home, college education, or your own comfortable retirement.

One of the most difficult aspects of a pastor's first-year finances is handling taxes. Because most pastors are self-employed, paying taxes suddenly becomes complicated. The IRS does not shy away from auditing pastors and churches, and unfortunately ignorance of the law is no excuse. Increasingly, pastors need the help of accounting professionals to untangle current tax laws concerning clergy.

If you cannot afford an accountant who is familiar with clergy tax preparation, some helpful resources are available. To begin, purchase or at least consult a good minister's tax and financial guide. It will help explain current tax laws and give you tips that can save money in future years. You might also consider investing in computer software that will help you keep track of your professional expenses and prepare your taxes as a self-employed clergy member. A few of the available resources are listed at the end of this chapter.

Your Church's Needs

Your church needs you as a pastor beyond the administrative responsibilities and preaching. There will be times when the church must come before your family. People will die on your day off. Members will have a crisis on the night you wanted to spend at home with your family. Operations will coincide with school and athletic events. While conflicts don't happen every week, they do happen.

Although some pastors have strict rules regarding their time off, flexibility is important here. I try to be away from home no more than three nights out of the week. While that isn't written in stone, I work at making two or three appointments in one evening, so I have fewer evenings away from my family.

Do you come back from vacation in an emergency? It depends on the situation. If the unexpected tragedy or a death affected many members, you might. Your decision may also depend on where you are vacationing; camping a few hours from home is different from being across the country. It is not always an easy task to find the balance that meets the needs of your church without sacrificing your family on its altar.

Like it or not, your family becomes a model for the church. When you carve out family time, people notice. When you model effective discipline techniques, other parents watch. When you hold hands with your spouse or scratch each other's backs during a fellowship dinner, other couples pay attention. Your church needs to see your family succeed.

In the same way, the church needs to see your family fail. Members need to know that your family is not perfect. When I confess to having grouchy, crabby Sunday mornings right before church, members understand. They're also a little relieved. Allowing your members to see your own family's foibles reminds them that no family is perfect.

Being a pastor requires more from your family than perhaps any other profession. It has its difficulties. The first time I walked into our den to find a member standing there because no one heard the knock and she just "knew" we were here, I was furious. But after I asked her not to do it again, she didn't.

Yet being a pastoral family is not without its great joys. Within the first month after we had arrived, an older woman with whom I was visiting told me, "I want you to know that I will be praying for you every single day that you are our pastor. You can depend on it." I have thanked God more than once for her prayers.

Being a pastor can be incredibly rewarding. Besides the personal and spiritual fulfillment, there are thoughtful gifts, notes of encouragements, garden produce, and lots of hugs. Many people in the congregation will become like a second family to you. My daughter has benefited greatly from families who have loved her and cared for her in a number of ways. Being a part of a church family is often one of the greatest benefits of being its pastor.

Resources

FAMILY

Clergy. Focus on the Family. (A magazine for pastors that addresses the particular needs of pastors and their families.)

Lorna Dobson, *I'm More Than the Pastor's Wife: Supporting Your Husband's Ministry without Losing Your Identity.* Zondervan Publishing House, 1995.

David and Vera Mace, *What's Happening with Clergy Marriages?* Abingdon Press, 1983.

FINANCES

Larry Burkett, *The Family Budget Workbook: Gaining Control of Your Personal Finances (revised edition).* Moody Press, 1993.

Daniel D. Busby, *The Zondervan Minister's Tax and Financial Guide 1998: For 1997 Tax Returns.* Zondervan Publishing House, 1998. (This book is revised every year or two.)

ClergyTax software, based on TurboTax Software. 1998.

David J. Epstein and J. David Epstein, *Clergy Tax 1998: A Tax Preparation Manual Developed for Clergy in Cooperation with IRS Tax Officials.* Regal Books, 1997.

Harold Moe, *Make Your Paycheck Last.* Harsand Press, 1993.

Jonathan P. Pond and Jonathan D. Pond, *1001 Ways to Cut Your Expenses.* Dell Books, 1992.

CHAPTER 9

Keeping the Well from Running Dry
How to Maintain Your Spiritual Life

Cultivation of personal spiritual growth is perhaps one of the most neglected areas of pastors' lives. We spend so much time caring for others' spiritual needs and concerns that our own spirituality gets left on the back burner. We have little extra time and even less energy. Besides, we spend hours reading the Bible and studying for classes and sermons, right?

Unfortunately, sermon and Bible study preparation does not go far toward nurturing a pastor's spiritual life. Many pastors are woefully undernourished when it comes to their own walks with God. Because pastors must try to balance family time with Bible study, sermon preparation, and other pastoral responsibilities, we often end up spending less time in prayer and devotions than many of our members do.

Pastors *need* to spend time alone with God. The demands

are too great and the stakes are too high for pastors to care for a body of people in the name of Christ, but not in his Spirit. Too many pastors spend hours and hours in preparation and administrative tasks and then ask God to bless their efforts after the fact. An important part of a devotional time is allowing time for God to direct our plans and problems.

A personal quiet time is absolutely essential for pastors for several reasons. First, we are encouraged and renewed when we have spent time with God. God the Sustainer can revive us. Second, giving God time to speak to us gives us clarity for our actions. Our Creator can give us wisdom. Lastly, when we are walking closely with our Lord, we are less likely to stray away from God's plan for our lives. The dangers of dishonesty and despair, infidelity and wrongdoing, are lessened. Our holy God can direct our paths.

Set Aside Time Daily

Setting aside a specific time period every day makes a quiet time easier to maintain. Otherwise, it gets too easily lost in a list of things that "have" to be done. All people have their own personal circadian rhythm and know what works best for them. For example, I am a morning person and do best when I do my devotions as soon as I get to the office, when no one else has arrived and all is quiet. Doing devotions at night is an exercise in futility for me because I am simply too tired to concentrate.

Once you have set time, remind yourself that this time belongs to God. When you become distracted and start thinking about your evening committee meeting, you are robbing time away from God. During the first few weeks of a regular devotional time, it may be difficult to pull away from all the distractions around you.

I find it helpful to keep a pad of paper and a pen nearby during devotional time. Then when something comes to mind that needs to be addressed later, you can write it down—briefly. That way, you know it will be remembered, and you can then give the time back to God and God's purposes.

Find a Specific Place

Everyone has a favorite place in the house. Look for the place where you will meet God. Your sacred space may be a quiet nook in the bedroom or out on the patio. Find a place that is sunny and well lit, that has a comfortable chair. You should enjoy being there. Doing your devotions in the same place helps maintain consistency.

In the same vein, keep your Bible and study guide in the same spot every day so you won't waste precious time looking for your materials. Keep everything, including a notebook and writing utensil, handy in a basket or other container nearby. If in the middle of receiving insight from God you have to go search for a pen, the moment can be lost.

While typically the church may not be the best place to go for quiet time, I find that with a young child in the house, church is often more quiet than my home. If you go early, you can be alone in the sanctuary before anyone else arrives. If a member does happen upon you there, it sets a good example for them to see the pastor in prayer. When I have done this, I have never been disturbed.

The church office can be adequate, but I find it offers many interruptions. If I can ignore the reports that need to be filled out and the list of people to call, then inevitably the phone will ring. Thus, for me, the office is not an ideal "sacred space." If, however, you are willing to unplug the phone or go in early and leave on the answering machine, you may be able to steal some quiet moments alone.

Keep a Prayer Journal

There are a number of good prayer notebooks and spiritual journals available. Some notebooks allow you to record prayer requests and then later note the ways that God has responded to prayer. Seeing God at work in such specific ways can be a real encouragement and provide continuing initiative to maintain good devotional habits.

For several months a few years ago, I had a prayer partner, and we began by writing down all of our prayer concerns so we could remember them during the week. After a few months of praying together, we began looking back and found that God had answered each prayer. While the answers were not always what we had specifically requested, God was faithful and brought resolution to each concern. What a blessing it was to see that God was continuously at work, especially when the results were not immediate.

Prayer notebooks can be used in a number of ways. You may prefer to record insights you receive from the Scripture or write down ways that God speaks to you as you meditate in silence. Remember, though, that this is meant to be a journal about your spiritual life and not an opportunity to write a sermon outline or design a Bible study series.

Use Scripture as Your Primary Resource

While other devotionals are useful, the primary resource for your devotional time is Scripture. Instead of focusing on how God's Word has spoken to others, allow it to speak to you. Be aware that it takes some effort to refocus one's Scripture reading to a meditative and reflective approach rather than an academic one.

What is God saying to you at this time in your life? What does the Scripture have to say about your situation, your hurts, your struggles? Read a passage several times, looking for things you may have never noticed before. Does this passage say something new to you or reinforce an idea you need to hear right now? Open yourself to hearing God's Word in a fresh way.

Add Other Devotionals

If you find that after spending time in prayer, meditation, and reading God's Word, you need more direction, devotionals are a helpful tool. Feel free to use them. In recent years an explosion of excellent devotionals has appeared in the Christian market. Many resources are designed specifically for people of a specific age or interest, and something is available for everyone. Most books are reasonably priced, and some computer programs now offer a devotional on your computer's daily planner.

Our Daily Bread and *The Upper Room* are two of the most popular daily devotionals that have been used by millions of readers for years. Some denominations offer their own versions. Such guides generally offer succinct stories, a thought for the day, and a short Scripture passage on which to meditate. I am surprised by how often a devotional reading will speak to what my heart needs at that moment.

If the guides are too contrived for you, there are literally hundreds of books on the market that can be read one chapter at a time. Some, like many of Max Lucado's works, have study questions at the end. If your devotional time is in a rut, this may be a good time to look at new resources, like those listed at the end of this chapter.

Other Sources for Spiritual Growth

Many pastors enjoy being a part of a spiritual-growth group. These groups can develop in a variety of forms, but they are not meant to replace a personal devotion time. Some pastors get together regularly to discuss a book or a specific topic as it relates to their own walks with God. Others have a personal prayer partner or spiritual mentor who encourages them and makes suggestions and recommendations for spiritual growth. In recent years, men's accountability groups have become more popular and provide excellent opportunities for male pastors to connect. Women may have to create their own support network of Christian women.

Don't Forget Prayer

Pastors are called to pray for many occasions. You'll be asked to offer grace at fellowship dinners and to pray at bedsides, in worship services, and even at public events like the opening of Little League season. Sometimes, so much time is spent in public corporate prayer that our own prayer life is sorely neglected.

If time allows for nothing else, use your devotional time for prayer. Nothing you can do is more important. Prayer allows you to hear God's word for your life, your family, and your congregation. It will not matter if you and your church are successful by the world's standards if you and the church are not being faithful to what God is calling you to do. Pray for:

- Your own walk with God and areas of sin that need God's cleansing
- Your family members and each of their needs
- God's wisdom for each of the church leaders
- Strength and insight for the Sunday school teachers and youth leaders
- Protection for the children and youth of the congregation
- Needs of the community, nation, and world
- Wisdom for how the church can spread the gospel to your community

Remember, too, to express in prayer your thankfulness for the ministry God has given you and the courage to be faithful to it.

Nurturing your spiritual life is too important to be left to chance. Setting aside an intentional time, place, and method will go a long way toward assuring that your walk with God will stay strong and healthy as you navigate the rough waters of your first church. Whatever approach works best differs from person to person, but we all need that time with our Lord.

God placed you where you are. Allow the Lord to continue to work in your life and in the lives of the members of the church by being open to God's plans. God put you there for a number of reasons. Staying in tune with God will enable you to be a part of the divine plan. Your church depends on your spiritual health. So do you.

Resources

Jackson W. Carroll, *As One with Authority: Reflective Leadership in Ministry*. Westminster John Knox Press, 1991.

Richard Foster, *Celebration of Discipline: The Path to Spiritual Growth*. Harper & Row, 1983.

Bill Hybels and Lavonne Neff, *Too Busy Not to Pray: Slowing Down to Be with God (revised edition)*. InterVarsity Press, 1998.

Henri J. M. Nouwen, *The Wounded Healer*. Doubleday, 1990.

CHAPTER 10

Reality Check
Taking Advice from the Trenches

You might as well learn this now—every church sincerely believes that it wants to grow and change, to be a church with a new direction. Every single committee that is in the business of hiring a new pastor will say so. They may even mean it. However, the painful truth is that many churches want to achieve growth with a minimum amount of pain, even less effort, and very little substantial change. Most members want growth as long as it means bringing in more people who are exactly like them and who don't try to sit in their pews.

Realizing that your church may not be exactly what you thought it was going to be is a painful realization. Probably no one lied to you, but perhaps the group misrepresented some information. Or, just as likely, their perspective on the current situation wasn't firmly grounded in reality. When you are confronted with the reality of whom God has given you as your flock, you may be tempted to throw in the towel.

Don't—not yet, anyway. In many ways, committing to a church family is similar to marriage. While you didn't exactly lie to your fiance(e) while you were dating, you also didn't reveal a few of your character flaws. How necessary was it to mention that your snoring could wake the dead or that your cooking skills barely exceed ripping open a package of pop-tarts? You didn't mean to be deceitful; you were just putting your best foot forward. And when the honeymoon is over, couples are forced to decide if they're going to go ahead and honor their commitments to each other, even if reality isn't exactly the package that they signed for.

Churches and pastors often find themselves in a similar predicament. When confronted with reality, often, as pastor, the most you can do is to pray for the church and its struggles. God was in that church before you got there, and God will be there after you leave. If God wants the doors to close, then that's what God will do. Your responsibility is not to build a mega-church but to be faithful to your calling as pastor. Face it, your church is probably not going to be another Willow Creek, but it doesn't have to be in order to build the kingdom of God.

Even if the church is deeply in debt or completely divided, the church where God has placed you is the right church at the right time for you. Don't forget that God is still at work. Commit your new ministry to prayer and be reminded that God is there and in the process of bringing redemption and grace to the areas that are lacking.

The time will also come when your congregation will realize that *you* are not all *they* had hoped you would be. You offended Aunt Sara by refusing second helpings of her infamous rhubarb-broccoli pie. Worse yet, you occasionally preach until three minutes after twelve, which allows the Baptists across the street to get a head start at the restaurant downtown. Alas, your members have discovered that you are not the perfect pastor.

Their first response may be to want to find a new pastor, the "right one" this time. But they will be learning that God is at work in you. They will be learning that the areas they see as concerns may be the areas where God is bringing redemption and grace in your life.

Perhaps God has brought you to this church to learn from them as well. Be willing to learn. Be teachable. Members are understanding if a difficult situation arises and you say honestly, "I'm new at this. I've not had to deal with this situation before. How can we solve this?" While you will have to shoot from the hip occasionally, enlisting the assistance and wisdom of others is rarely a bad decision. Very few people expect you to have all the answers.

Above all, be real. Be the person God has created you to be. You are probably never going to be as charismatic as the pastor down the road or as silver-tongued as another colleague, but the Lord has given you gifts and talents designed to bring honor and glory to God. Be faithful to what God has given.

Dealing with Conflict

Unfortunately, some people are mean, petty, and unkind. You probably have people in your church who have disliked every pastor that has ever served, and they may say you are no better than the worst of your predecessors. I have heard it said that the church is not a museum for saints but a hospital for sinners. Your church is no different. Your congregation will be full of people whom God loves and seeks to change.

Effective ministry depends on pastors having the ability to identify and work with potentially explosive people and situations. Diplomacy and skills in conflict resolution are absolutely critical. Every church will have people with whom you will disagree, and if you are unable to handle them, you will have short pastorates.

This is not to deny that personal criticism can be difficult to receive—especially because it is rarely offered to you personally! What often happens instead is that someone will relay to you what another member has said. Remembering a few general guidelines will help you deal with these situations.

First, seriously listen to what is being said; do not be defensive. Thank the person for his or her concern and communicate your intention to consider what you have heard. Then *do* it. Think about the criticism, and decide if the comment is a petty personal attack or if it is a legitimate concern that needs to be addressed. Don't neglect to consider the source. When someone comes to me with a minor complaint, I evaluate my relationship with that person first. Know your people well enough to discern whether something else might be going on to spark conflict. I try to remember when I last visited the person. Is the criticism an attempt to get my attention because of a sense of neglect? You may want to go back to the person and ask for clarification of the concern or for assistance in resolving the difficulty.

When in doubt, seek input from your spouse or a leader in the church whom you trust. That individual can help hold you accountable if the concern is a legitimate one. As painful as it is, we need to be reprimanded and corrected some-times. We all drop the ball on one occasion or another. Do not be too proud to acknowledge your errors and to ask for forgiveness when needed. Once, I forgot to visit someone whose family member was undergoing serious surgery. By the time I remembered, she was angry and hurt. Forgive-ness took time, and the experience was humbling. I have not made that mistake with anyone since.

On the other hand, don't worry about putting out every single little fire. Ask God for wisdom to discern how to handle inevitable conflicts. Keep your sense of humor. I have been criticized for everything from wearing white shoes after Labor Day to keeping the sanctuary too cold. Working with and loving the people of God is no easy challenge, but bringing healing and hope to relationships is worth the effort. Your example offers a powerful model to your members.

Finding Friendships

I loved my new church. I loved being pastor. The people were warm, open, and kind. I had it all: a great family, fulfilling marriage, and flourishing career. I was also des-perately lonely. Having left behind several close friends when I moved, I discovered that the biggest adjustment I had to make at my new church was finding friends. I was not alone. That sense of isolation and loneliness is a com-mon problem for clergy. Although we are surrounded by people and relationships, many pastors complain of too few genuine friendships. The pastorate is often a solitary place to be.

God created us to be in community. We were created to be in close relationships. We feel alone when we don't have someone with whom to share ourselves and our experiences. Without those friendships, pastors are prone to burnout, depression, and health problems.

A lack of close friendships and a good support system also makes pastors more susceptible to an inappropriate relationship with individual members of the congregation. Tread carefully when making close friendships within the church. Relationships that appear to be exclusive within the church may create jealousy among other members.

Pastors need to take action to dispel the feeling of isolation and loneliness. First, realize that you are responsible for creating friendships. Instead of feeling sorry for yourself and waiting for new friends to fall in your lap, begin to look around and see who your acquaintances are. Go ahead and make the initial move to strengthen those budding relationships, and see if there is the potential for greater intimacy.

Second, broaden your horizons. Being involved with other pastors in their denominations and communities may be helpful. Many communities have clergy groups that meet monthly for fellowship and to plan special events. Besides finding professional colleagues, pastors may find friendships among those who share similar struggles. Particularly for young female clergy, companionship with other women pastors may be lifesaving.

Pastors need to have lives beyond their own church walls. There are times when life in the church can be stressful, and it is helpful to be able to get away from it all. Realize that you need to become more involved in interests outside the church that will allow you to become acquainted with more people. Friendships can be made at the gym, at a craft class, at a Rotary club meeting. Community involvement allows the opportunity for pastors both to develop in other areas of their lives and to meet new people. Additionally, you can reach more people with the gospel with whom you wouldn't come into contact otherwise.

Finding a Mentor

The one thing that helped the most in my first year of ministry as a senior pastor was having a mentor that I trusted and respected. As I had questions about counseling, job evaluations, funeral planning and more, my former senior pastor was an excellent source of wisdom and insight. His support made the first few months much easier. Because it was a long-distance relationship, we communicated by phone, and more frequently, by e-mail. I would recommend cultivating a mentoring relationship close to home if it is possible. Mentors can be of great assistance for professional, personal, and spiritual guidance.

Pray about it, observe local pastors you know, and consider asking for their assistance. Most pastors with a few years under their belts are more than happy to take new pastors under their wings. Take advantage of the extra support; it can make a world of difference.

How Long Should You Stay?

Many new pastors ask how long they should stay at their first pastorates and how they will know when to leave. One pastor suggests that it is time to go when someone places a U-Haul gift certificate in your mailbox or when the health insurance plan your church offers lists the primary healthcare provider as Dr. Kevorkian. Unfortunately, rarely is the decision that clear.

Some pastors stay for a few years and then move on to churches with larger paychecks and more opportunities.

Others stay at their first churches for decades. And the rest of us fall somewhere in the middle, struggling to balance the desire to succeed professionally with the desire to stay with a church long-term to see it change and grow.

No right answer fits everyone. If a pastor has only been at church for three or four years and wants to move on, then examine carefully the reasons for that desire. Is the church in a real stretching period where it needs consistent leadership to sustain a period of growth? Who is initiating the question of moving—the pastor or the church? If the latter, is it the entire board or one vocal critic? Why is the question being raised? What is the motive or impetus behind the urge to move on? Without clearly understanding the need for a move, the pattern may be repeated by the church and the pastor every few years.

There are times when it is appropriate to leave a church within a few years. More often, however, the church needs a pastor to be willing to stay and help the congregation work through the current bump in the road. Staying with a difficult pastorate can be an opportunity to model faithfulness, even through tough times. At other times, though, God's call is clear and we must say good-bye again.

Ultimately, God has a plan for you and for your church. Work with the church leaders at seeking God's will for all concerned. In times of difficulty, remember to spend extra time on your knees, practicing good discipleship. You can deal with difficult situations when you have the assurance that you are where God wants you to be. When you are no longer sure of that, your current position becomes a difficult place to be.

Being a pastor is one of the most challenging and rewarding callings a person can ever hope to undertake. I am frequently surprised at the depth of my feeling for the people that God has given me to nurture. That feeling is a precious gift from God to pastors who are willing to open their hearts to it. What a blessing to feel God's love flow through you to the people you have been called to shepherd!

When a pastor is invited to walk with a couple struggling through the early years of marriage or helping a family prepare for death, God is there. Clergy are honored to have the opportunity to stand with people as babies are dedicated, marriages are begun, and loved ones are laid to rest. We are incredibly blessed to be allowed to connect people with the love and grace and mercy of God.

But make no mistake, you will know days of darkness also. Times will come when you are discouraged and feel like a failure. The church consists of hurting people who will, at times, lash out at you. That too is part of being a member of the body of Christ.

In those times, especially, know that you do not walk alone. Be reminded that the One who called you will not forsake you. The Lord will be faithful. You belong to God.

Resources

George Barna, ed., *Leaders on Leadership: Wisdom, Advice, and Encouragement on the Art of Leading God's People*. Regal Books, 1998.

Jack W. Hayford, *Pastors of Promise: Pointing to Character and Hope as the Keys to Fruitful Shepherding (Hayford Pastors Series)*. Regal Books, 1997.

Gary Inrig, *Quality Friendship*. Moody Press, 1988.